Ukraïner

Ukrainian Insider

Lviv
The Old Lion Publishing House
2019

Introduction

Ukraïner began as an attempt to express what characterized Ukraine to the people I met as I traveled around the world. I found myself describing my country and hometown — or at the very least their locations — to children on the remote islands of the Indonesian archipelago, Bedouins in the Arabian desert, grandparents at a Polish seniors' club, tourist groups, and international festival goers. Over the years of traveling through various parts of the world, I realized that what my talks about Ukraine lacked most was an emotion — something that would make a lasting impression on those I spoke with and remain forever associated in their memory with my homeland. At the time, Ukraine's image abroad was primarily defined by football players, political jokes, and disasters. After I returned home from my journeys around the world, I wanted to find a description of this modern-day country; a short but eloquent answer to the question "Where are you from?"

In June 2016, a group of other like-minded people and I set off on an adventure, or as we decided to call it, an expedition. We announced our idea to explore Ukraine and unveil it to the world on social media. Within a few days we received hundreds of messages and several thousand subscribers. With this, our multimedia project Ukraïner was launched.

At the very beginning of our expedition we realized how little we knew about our own country. So we had set off for a different historical region every month for two and a half years, learning the stories and daily lives of active and engaged citizens to highlight their valuable contributions to Ukraine, whether they were in the most remote corners of the country or in the largest cities.

We hoped publishing our material would gradually erode away internal borders that had formed over the years from stereotypes, fears, and media coverage. The very names of some regions — Donbas, Halychyna, Volyn — for many Ukrainians bore negative connotations irrespective of the reality in those areas. We understood our vital mission as two fold: first, to break down these internal borders, and second, to turn the locals into heroes and central focus of our stories. We expressed value in things that locals had taken for granted by creating new images of their homes as a way of re-discovering histories and places. We aimed to re-discover histories and places, express value for things that locals took for granted, and by doing so help depict these localities in a new light.

For some of the people, Ukraïner provided an opportunity to re-evaluate their lives. We listened to their stories about themselves, creating a space for them to see the value of their activities. Their sense of pride in their work grew.

At the beginning of our project we had a few dozen volunteers helping with the project. This has grown to the point where we currently have several hundred involved in the further development of the project. Everyone has been involved in realizing the goal to document our expedition, dedicating their time to help share the real Ukraine: writers, editors, and transcribers have worked on the text; directors, film editors, and producers have provided the video material; and translators made it possible to publish our stories in several languages; the travelers and explorers; diplomats; and media and communications experts.

This book is only one part of the larger multimedia project available at **ukrainer.net**. It contains stories collected from each region, full versions of which can be found with the use of the QR code.

Bogdan Logvynenko

Contents

Zakarpattia

Michel and his Buffaloes

The ecologist Michel Jacobi came to Ukraine from Germany to preserve Ukraine's ecosystem and traditional stock-breeding practices .

Despite the fact that modern animal husbandry norms prefer cows and intensive farming practices, Michel began to breed buffaloes. In the early 20th century, raising buffalo was common in Zakarpattia; there were several thousand buffaloes in the neighboring villages. When the communists came to power they placed all the buffaloes in collective farms. But the female buffaloes did not like their new conditions in the collective farms and stopped producing milk. By the 1990s, the buffalo population declined from a few thousand to around one hundred.

— I thought that in Ukraine I could find the same natural environment and lifestyle of our ancestors since they don't exist in Germany anymore. People need to live in harmony with nature. I want to show this by my own example.

With the support of a few charity foundations and a few village leaders who gave him a leftover land that once belonged to the collective farms, Michel began collecting his buffalo herd from the surrounding areas.

Michel watches over his herd at farms in Chumaliovo and Steblivka and works on a breed registry. Michel also ensures that his buffaloes also live in the semi-wild shores of the Danube.

Mount Yavirnyk. Yanko Derevlianyi

Artist, sculptor, and architect Yanko Derevlianyi, looking for a place to live in harmony with nature, chose Yavirnyk, a mountain near the town of Velykyi Bereznyi, to set up his workshop. Yanko first came to Yavirnyk in 1974 when he was working as an interior-designer at Soviet-era tourist complex. Since then he has been very active in the area designing and building huts and fire-pits for travelers.

— Even cats run wild on the mountain, and it's a rare soul that can spend much time here.

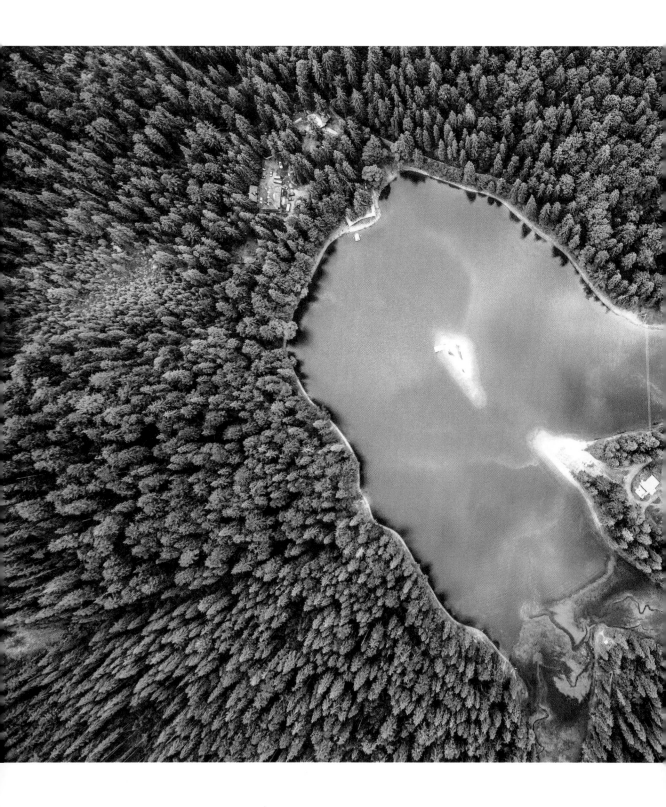

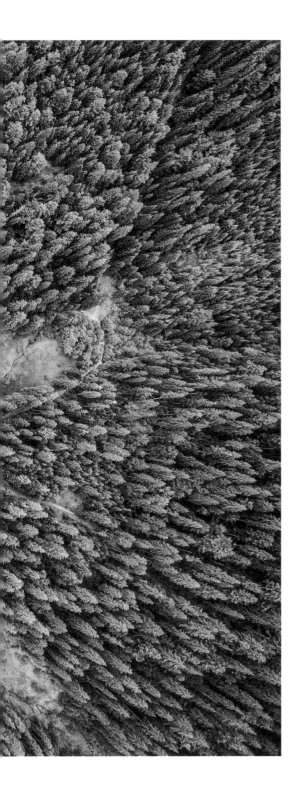

Synevyr is the largest mountain lake in Ukraine, located at an elevation of 989 metres above sea level in the Vnutrishni (Inner) Gorgany mountain range in the Carpathians.

Borzhava Narrow-Gauge Railway

Locals call the Borzhava narrow-gauge railway, built at the beginning of the 20th century, by its diminutive name 'Antsia'. The train is drawn by an old diesel locomotive TU-2, produced in the 1950s. Vynohradiv train station is one of the favourite meeting points for the locals that also hosts a market.

Antsia is only one of a few active narrow-gauge railways in Ukraine, with a rail width of 750 millimetres. Its route, from Vynohradiv through Khmilnyk to Irshava, is 123 kilometres long. The main rail goes along the Borzhava River, from which the name of the railway comes from. The two carriages and the old locomotive cross the market in Vynohradiv carrying the passengers through Zakarpattia.

Valentyn Kuzan 17

In the 1930s, the village Kolochava was mentioned in the novel Nikola the Outlaw, by Czech author Ivan Olbracht who had lived there for several years. The book made Kolochava village a rather popular destination for Czech tourists. Nowadays, Kolochava offers many museums and an unforgettably picturesque road along the river leading to the village.

Vlachs

Vlachs are an ethnic group living all over Central and Southeast Europe. The majority of the Vlachs in Ukraine live in villages throughout Zakarpattia and Bessarabia. Living in relatively closed communities, they are primarily woodworkers and shepherds. One of their shepherds' huts is near Mount Pidpula, part of the Svydovets massif in the Carpathians. For a few months every year, the Vlachs graze their flocks here and cook traditional meals from fresh dairy products.

Carolling in Dovhe

Traditional koliada-singing (carolling) is performed on the 7th and 8th of January in Dovhe, Zakarpattia.

Older boys dress up as shepherds and one is designated to be an old man. The youngest boys, dressed as angels, have the hardest mission: carrying the wooden "vertep" (Transl. A 'vertep' is a portable puppet theatre) called a "betlehem" in the local dialect. It is very heavy, and with each house the children pass they get more and more tired. The boys are supposed to switch who carries the vertep every five houses, but they often lose count.

Older boys don't have it easy, either. The costumes are uncomfortable, the text is easy to forget, and they need to make it through the younger children's constant arguing. But they are at least treated to some homemade alcohol after they carol at a house. As the "responsible one", the 'old man' can't drink. The 'shepherds' on the other hand don't mind indulging themselves from time to time.

The Roma of Korolevo

One-third of the Roma in Ukraine live in densely populated settlements in Zakarpattia. Ukraine is home for some 40,000 Roma, in accordance with the data from NGOs working with Roma population. The compact Roma settlements in Zakarpattia are designed as residential areas with separate streets, quarters, or neighbourhoods.

The population of the Korolevo settlement in Vynohradiv district is over 3,700 people. This is one of the best planned Roma settlements in Zakarpattia. The houses are made of bricks here, and sometimes they are even multi-storied. The roads are graveled. The kids running around on the streets are clean, and the girls wear traditional Roma dresses.

Clothing is very important status symbol for the women. Skirts are embroidered with gold and silver goldwork, and clothes are decorated with glass jewellery. Family jewellery is often very valuable and usually custom-made. These family jewels will serve as the a dowry for a bride, a symbol of her family's prosperity.

Men from Korolevo work in teams consisting of close relatives and neighbours. Together they make the parts for tin roofs and rain gutters. Craftsmen here have a long-standing reputation and their own adornment style.

Pryazovia

A dried-up football field in the village Hryhorivka.

Askania-Nova

Askania-Nova is the biggest in Europe and the oldest steppe biosphere reserve in the world. It has been listed in the UNESCO World Network of Biosphere Reserves since 1984.

In 1898, the German Friedrich Falz-Fein gave the first 600 hectares of land to the reserve. As a researcher, he wanted to observe how nature would develop without human interference. He had been spending a significant share of his income on development of a zoo and preservation of the steppe reserve.

Viktor Havrylenko, the managing director of Askania-Nova, knows every square metre of these lands. Only his car is allowed to enter the reserve as it's the only one the wild animals are used to.

— I tell my colleagues that I am the wildest among them. Nobody has lived in the forest, away from any kind of human settlement, longer than I have.

Nowadays, Askania-Nova's ecosystem includes more than 500 plant species and over 3,000 animal species. Here you can study the behaviour of zebras, bison, and antelopes in semi-wild environment very similar to their natural habitats.

Serhiy Korovayny 31

Berdiansk

He had been spending a significant share of his income on development of a zoo and preservation of the steppe reserve. The Soviet era railway tracks running right along the waterfront have become the iconic image of the town.

Botieve and Bulgarians

Pryazovia is a multicultural region. Bulgarians, Greeks, Albanians, Germans, and many other nationalities have co-existed here for centuries.

The ethnic Bulgarian community in Pryazovia emerged after a wave of immigration lasting from 1861 to 1862. Coming from Bessarabia, these Bulgarian settlers founded more than 30 villages.

During the 1990s, many societies of the Bulgarian culture have been established. As a result of their efforts, folk bands were formed and Bulgarian was

introduced both at schools and in newspapers. We see hope for the future of the Bulgarian language and traditions in Pryazovia precisely because the preserved Bulgarian culture here has such a unique and distinctive character.

Mariupol. Slag Heaps

Mariupol, the city of factories and the sea, is located in the south-east of Ukraine. About 100,000 people out of the city's half a million work at local factories.

Slag heaps, piled from the heavy industry factories leftovers have become the landmarks of the city. Huge hills of draw rocks are usually located near factories.

Earlier during the Russian-Ukrainian armed conflict, there was a time when Mariupol was under occupation. Immediately after the Ukrainian government took back control, Mariupol began investing in new infrastructure projects, from new coworking spaces and playgrounds to concert and theatre halls. This allows to prepare the city for eventual closure of the heavy industries by developing new sectors and broadening labor market. Hopefully, the strategy will cushion possible economic decrease and give the city the new impulse.

Novovasylivka. The Molokans

The religious community of the Molokans is a branch of Spiritual Christianity, though the traditional church claims them to be a sect. These Christians spread to Pryazovia from Russia in the 18th century. Molokans were fleeing the Empire to reach its borderlands in order to preserve their religion based on old rituals.

Molokans differ from Russian Orthodox church members: they don't have icons, they consume milk during lent, and they don't accept sacraments. Their religious traditions are very simple: they sing spiritual songs and listen to preachings during their prayer meetings.

People know very little about Molokans, although the most famous centre of this Old Believer consociation is located in the village Novovasylivka, Pryazovia.

Photographer Oleksandr Prykhnenko

Oleksandr Prykhnenko is a shipbuilder, writer, and
photographer from the town Henichesk. Oleksandr
has accomplished much in his 80 years: he has visited several dozens countries, published 26 books,
and filmed a documentary.

Kamiana Mohyla

Kamiana Mohyla is a unique rock formation in the middle of the Pryazovia steppe. From above, this hill of boulders resembles the human brain. Long ago people believed that unusual natural landmarks like these were endowed with mystical properties and would treat them as outdoor shrines.

Rock carvings from different epochs can be found in the grottos and caves of Kamiana Mohyla. The carvings have lost their definition with time since they were carved on the soft surface of sandstone. Today the place is shrouded in legend.

Dmytro Okhrimenko   45

Poltavshchyna

Carpet Manufacture in Reshetylivka

Reshetylivka town is one of the historical centres of carpet manufacturing in Ukraine. It has been known for its master artisans since the 19th century. Reshetylivka developed as a centre of arts and crafts owing to the high-quality fine wool from a local breed of sheep and its unique embroidery and weaving techniques. Even though mechanization and commercialization are steadily superseding the local businesses and traditional methods, there are still several carpet manufacturers in Reshetylivka.

In the Soviet times, artists from all over the USSR would come to Reshetylivka, just like Yevhen and Larysa Piliuhin did. The talented couple were offered a job at the local college as folk art specialists. The Piliuhins continue to develop the art and industry of carpet making and work to ensure that their skills are passed onto the next generation.

Horishni Plavni. Vasyl Leshchenko — The Yachtsman

Horishni Plavni is an industrial town on the banks of the Kamianske Reservoir. Several villages were demolished for the construction of the mineral processing plant. The town is named after the wetlands, called "plavni" in Ukrainian, that encircle the town. The water recreation area incentivized the development of amateur yachting and even a shipbuilding yard. Back in the 1970s, a yacht club was founded in Horishni Plavni. The club eventually turned into the town's hallmark.

Vasyl Leshchenko has built about ten yachts in his garage. His yacht "Frigate" is now one of the town's symbols. Vasyl's interest in shipbuilding began with model wooden boats.

— In 1972, I bought a simple wooden boat for 10 rubles and used ordinary bedsheets for the sails. We used to sail on this little boat with my family whenever we went swimming.

Taras Kovalchuk   51

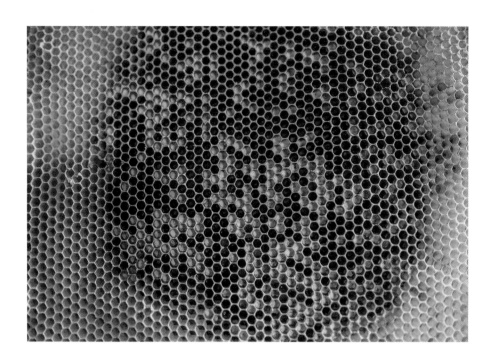

Yuryivka. Ivan Hura — The Beekeeper

Yuryivka is so small no one ever bothered to mark the way to it with the signpost. What was once a populous village with over 60 households and about 300 residents is now home to fewer than 20 people. Despite this, Yuryivka boasts the largest apiary in the region with over 100 beehives. Ivan Hura manages the whole production. If it were not for the apiary, the village would very likely no longer even exist.

— Once, at an alumni reunion, my former classmates asked, "Who is that idiot who settled down in Yuryivka?" I replied proudly, "I am!"

54

Potters of Opishne

There are about ten pottery centres in Ukraine and Opishne in Poltavshchyna is the largest among them. This area is rich in clay deposits. From the end of the 19th century to the beginning of the 20th century, one out of three families here worked in pottery.

The great variety of shapes and sizes in ceramics emerged to complement the needs of Ukraine's many culinary dishes and diverse cultural traditions.

Opishne's traditional pottery painting is characterized by floral motifs such as flowers, grapes, wheat ears, and branches. Warm red and brown hues are accented by touches of green and blue.

Panasivka. Valerii Yermakov

Panasivka is a village located on the left bank of the Psel River in Poltavshchyna near Myrhorod. Finding Panasivka on the map requires some effort and no public transport goes to the town. There are no more than 20 people living in the village now. Those who do find their way here will see a Ukrainian flag fluttering next to the Panasivka sign. It indicates that this place is the home of Valerii Yermakov, a sculptor and artist.

Prior to Ukraïner's expedition visit, Valerii was virtually unknown. However, he admits that fame was never something he wanted to pursue. Valerii has been living a solitary life since his wife died a few years ago. At age 79, Valerii is one of the youngest men in the village. He has turned his yard into an open-air gallery for his peculiar sculptures. Valerii admires Nikolai Gogol (whose famous story "The Fair at Sorochyntsi" is set within 10 km from here)

and Greek mythology. Having no formal art education nor life models, he uses only magazines as a guide.

— People strive for material wealth. I, on the other hand, only want to be able to create, and to have enough strength and courage.

After meeting Valerii, we came up with the idea to arrange a trip to Greece for him and make a movie about it. The Ukraïner team applied to several companies to support this project but none of them showed interest in it. We decided to raise necessary funds to realize Valerii's dream by launching a fundraising campaign on Facebook. Almost 850 people donated around $4,000 USD in total and made Valerii's dream come true.

Serhiy Korovayny   59

Pavlo Pashko, Mykola Nosok

A Journey from Panasivka to Greece

In March 2018, sculptor Valerii Yermakov travelled abroad for the first time in his life. His journey through Greece, a country that had inspired him since childhood, lasted for 11 days. His specially planned itinerary focused on exploring Athens, Delphi, and Peloponnese peninsula.

Following his return to Ukraine, Valerii held his very first press conference. He spoke about Ukrainian and Greek people he had met on his trip, among which were the mayors of Olympia and Zacharo. He described the museums he had visited and reflected on his experience in Greece, a country he once only dreamed about from books and films. At home in Panasivka, Valerii made a private presentation for his fellow villagers. Valerii fastened a Greek flag near the Ukrainian one next to Panasivka road sign.

Kriachkivka. Jurij Fedynskyj

Jurij Fedynskyj was born into a family of Ukrainian immigrants in the USA. At age 23, Jurij moved to Ukraine, but views it as coming home rather than moving.

As a child Jurij came across a pre-war recording of bandura players in his family's collection. The melodies and the voice touched him. After this introduc-

tion to Ukrainian culture, he became interested in kobzars (wandering folk bards) art, Ukrainian music, and folk instruments. Jurij received a degree in music in Detroit and after that travelled across the USA performing Ukrainian music.

He would later continue his studies in Ukraine, receiving his second degree.

— It is safe to say that I came back home 250 years after the destruction of the Zaporizhian Cossack Sich.

Jurij Fedynskyj and his wife Maria have built a workshop for musical instruments in Kriachkivka. Much was lost during the Soviet era in terms of traditional musical instruments making, sound and playing.

Jurij and Maria work to restore what was lost. Their newly built village house has a studio with several dozen traditional instruments — kobzas, banduras, torbans, lyres, and husli (an instrument belonging to the zither family).

Polissia

The Singing of Polissia

Polissia is famous for its authentic singing techniques with a great number of voice range switching. The singing is an integral part of work, leisure, traditional ceremonies and rites.

There is neither a village hall nor a shop in Svalovychi village, and a truck delivers bread there just once a week. Kateryna Trush lives here alone in her house — her husband died a long time ago and her children moved out.

— You can walk through Svalovychi, and you won't find anyone who can sing you the way I do! They send everyone to me because nobody can sing old songs the way I can.

If you ask Kateryna how many songs she knows, she will answer with a smile, 'A hundred thousand and one!'

The singing usually involves two to three voices. Although the number of villagers is decreasing, there are still some locals here who remember and preserve the songs. The singing of Polissia attracts both Ukrainians and foreigners who want to learn this unique art.

Wild honey Farmers from Kniazivka

Wild honey farming (bortnytstvo) is an old practice of harvesting honey from wild bees. Many sources considered this practice to be lost on the territory of Ukraine in the 18th and 19th centuries. However, wild honey hunters still exist in Polissia.

The name of this craft originates from wooden logs where bees live — 'borts'. Hollow logs, cut off with an axe, are hung up on trees as high as possible.

Such positioning contributes to the unique taste of honey, gathered from the first blossoming in spring to the late flowers in autumn.

Yurii and Tetiana Starynski from Kniazivka village inherited the art of bortnytstvo from their parents. They wish their children also followed their family business. They are the last wild honey farmers in this village.

— This activity calms me down. Anything can happen in this life due to stress. When I feel stressed, I just go to my bees, stand next to their beehive, and let everything go just watching them.

Serhiy Korovayny   69

Antonivka-Zarichne Narrow-Gauge Railway

The Antonivka-Zarichne narrow-gauge railway has been operating for over 115 years. The locals call it 'Polissia tram', or 'Kukushka' ('a cuckoo'). For some villages along the route, it is the only transport available. The train passes by the wooden and metal bridge over the Styr River. This bridge is unique for Ukraine. The railroad starts from Antonivka town and stretches 106 kilometres to Zarichne. This is the longest narrow-gauge railroad in Europe.

Cows at the pasture near Mlynok village.

The Self-Settlers of Chornobyl

On the night on April 26, 1986, the disaster at the Chornobyl Nuclear Power Plant occurred. Only after several days did authorities inform the population about the scale of the catastrophe and started evacuation. People were forcibly relocated from the territories now known as the "Exclusion Zone".

When the level of contamination of the territory was officially announced, the majority of evacuated people feared to return to their homes. Almost everyone stayed in their new places. Everyone but self-settlers.

The majority of them, driven by homesickness, returned during the first year after the accident. Even militaries and barbwire could not stop them. Some of them did not leave the territory at all. They hid from the military in barns or cellars and ignored

evacuation notices. Also, those who worked on the Chornobyl Nuclear Power Plant and its subsidiaries remained in the Zone 'by default'. They used to get temporary passes, which were required to be renewed annually.

The villagers of the Chornobyl Exclusion Zone call themselves 'self-settlers', jokingly though, as that is actually their home.

The Chornobyl Exclusion Zone

The Exclusion Zone emerged after the Chornobyl Nuclear Power Plant disaster. First, it was a totally restricted area, even for those who lived there. Nowadays, it is a very popular tourist destination.

The town of Prypiat, located just two kilometres away from the nuclear power plant, is a monument of human negligence. It is abandoned and contaminated by radiation. With no human activity around,

forest took over the area. This space is inhabited by wild animals, and their population is constantly growing. At the same time, it could be a potential town-museum of international level, a monument to the enormous technogenic catastrophe.

Another popular destination nearby is 'Duha' ('an arch'), a radar complex built in the 1970s as a large-scale air defence project, a part of the Cold War

arms race. This secret complex had cost the USSR almost twice as much as the construction of the Chornobyl Nuclear Power Plant, though never launched into regular operation. After the Chornobyl disaster, 'Duha' was decommissioned , and gradually became a tourist point of interest.

Pavlo Pashko, Oleksandr Khomenko

Hoich Hamlet

The hamlet Zelenyi Hai is located 120 kilometres from Kyiv. The old-timers call it Hoich, which means 'forest clearing' in the local dialect. The hamlet has only 11 houses. The journalist from Kyiv, Kateryna Mizina, has bought one of them. Gradually she turned this place into an art space. Together with friends, she organizes festivals, movie screenings, and art projects.

— People often have no space to get to know each other, to talk, to work, to dig the soil, to polish wood, and so on. Occupational therapy can be a wonderful thing indeed. The air is excellent here as well as the conditions: there is neither the Internet nor good phone signal here. This brings people together — they unplug and start communicating.

Taras Kovalchuk   79

Mykola and Tetiana Vaskevych from the village Komory hold their youth photo. The couple preserves the local tradition of singing. Previously, everyone used to sing in Komory but nowadays, less than 40 residents remain in the village, and most of them are in their seventies or older.

Quarries of Korostyshiv

Korostyshiv is famous for massive extraction and processing of granite. Nowadays, hundreds of small entrepreneurs use the premises of the former Soviet enterprises to process large granite blocks. The deposits of granite in the area are still impressive. The old quarries, though, have become tourist attractions. Former deposit extraction places get filled with water.

The most popular flooded quarry is shaped like a horseshoe and has a deep lake in the middle. Its rocky banks are covered with pines, firs, and birches. The overhanging cliffs above the water have become the training place for climbers.

Bessarabia

Pelicans

The biggest population of white pelicans (Pelecanus onocrotalus) resides in the Danube Delta, between the territories of Ukraine and Romania.

Sheep Breeders

Sheep breeding is quite common in the steppe areas of Southern Ukraine and in the mountainous areas of the Carpathians. In Bessarabian villages, local ethnic groups of Bulgarians, Gagauz, and Moldovans are usually engaged in sheep breeding. Sheep breeding traditions differ quite often from village to village abundantly scattered all over the region.

Serhiy Korovayny, Oleksandr Ratushnyak 89

Vylkove. A Town on the Water

Vylkove is a unique Ukrainian town located in the Danube estuary where the river enters the Black Sea. For a long time, local people have been moving around through the channels called 'yeryks'. Yeryks, sadly, are being filled up and turned into roads for cars. People use motor boats or ordinary boats where they sail with a single oar standing in a boat. There are also pedestrian wooden pavements along the canals.

Frumushyka-Nova

Frumushyka-Nova is a contemporary replication of the village that had been founded here in the 18th century and was completely demolished due to the building of a gunnery range in the Soviet times. In 2006, the Palariievs family started restoring the village in accordance with the mapping records. They established a museum and recreation complex, as well as one of the largest sheep farms in Europe.

The tallest world monument of a shepherd was also erected here. The 16.4-metre monument has already been registered in the Guinness World Records.

— This monument costs as much as a kilometre of road pavement. We need 18 kilometres of road to be paved. Doesn't it make sense to create an object worth paving a road to?

Tourists come to Frumushyka-Nova to take a look at another unique object in Ukraine — the open-air museum of socialist realism. In the middle of the steppe, one can find over a hundred sculptures depicting leaders of the Soviet epoch. Lenin, Brezhnev, Stalin, Chkalov, Kirov, and Chapayev meet sunrises and see off sunsets which are just incredible in this area.

The Tuzly Estuaries

The Tuzly Estuaries National Park is a chain of 13 estuaries in the interfluve area of rivers Danube and Dnister. The core of the park is comprised of the salty estuaries Shahany, Alibey, Burnas, and some other smaller lagoons. The estuaries are separated from the Black Sea by a 36-kilometre barrier spit.

The territory of the park has encapsulated all the variety of local flora and fauna — you can see more than 300 kinds of birds and 40 kinds of animals, and the waters contain around 60 kinds of fish.

Pavlo Pashko   95

The Winemaker Lacarin from Shabo

Christophe Lacarin de Fabiani is a French entrepreneur, perfumer, and winemaker. He grows 14 varieties of grape on the shore of the Dnister Estuary. In 2016, he received a licence and an excise stamp to produce wine. He makes wine manually and without any chemical additives. His love for animals encouraged him to fill his homestead up with goats, chickens, horses, and sheep. In Shabo, monsieur Lacarin has found a perfect place for both work and life — with great soils, mild climate, and fresh air.

— Life isn't just about work, is it? One cannot think about money all the time. Be happy. Enjoy life.

Zatoka

Zatoka is a popular resort in the Odesa region.

Its southern side is located on Budzhak spit that separates the Black Sea and the Budzhak estuary. The rest of the settlement is situated on Karolino-Buhaz spit between the Black Sea and the Dnister Estuary.

After the annexation of Crimea by Russia, Zatoka beach attracts more and more tourists.

Serhiivka. The Yachting School

Serhiivka is a resort settlement not far from Odesa that became the centre of yachting. It is located on the shore of the Budzhak estuary. Students of the yachting school founded by Viacheslav and Oleksandr Smetanka practice here. First international competitions took place in Serhiivka in the 1990s. Viacheslav Smetanka also dreams to organize yachting courses for children from other regions of Ukraine.

— We have everything here: hot water, therapeutic mud, a lot of fish, and pelicans that have chosen Ukraine as their native land and always come back to us. We want our children to grow and live here, not leave for somewhere else.

Utkonosivka: the Tomato Cultivating Valley

The tomato growing valley in Bessarabia is called Utkonosivka village. It has 4,000 residents, and the majority of them grow vegetables, mainly tomatoes. Growing a particular kind of tomato called 'Primadonna' is a distinctive feature of the village. This tomato is recognizable due to a beak-looking tip, so-called 'nose'. Another unique feature of the village is a greenhouse in every homestead.

Until 1947, the village was called Ördek-Burnu, translated from the Nogai language as 'a duck's beak'. Take a look at a map, and you will see that the outline of the village resembles a duck. The modern name of the village — Utkonosivka (literally 'a duck's nose') — is a result of a wordplay and a translation pun. The village is located near the Katlabukh lake. It is 16 kilometres from the Danube and 50 kilometres from the Black Sea and the Danube Delta Biosphere Reserve.

The Buffaloes from Orlivka

The village Orlivka is surrounded with water. The Danube reed beds wash it on one side, and a number of big lakes - on the other. The straits get overgrown with reeds and covered with silt, and the land gets flooded. Black buffaloes help to save local ecosystem. The ecologist Michel Jacobi brought here one of his herds from Zakarpattia. The buffaloes are well adjusted to climate changes; they graze plants from the local water, helping to clean them.

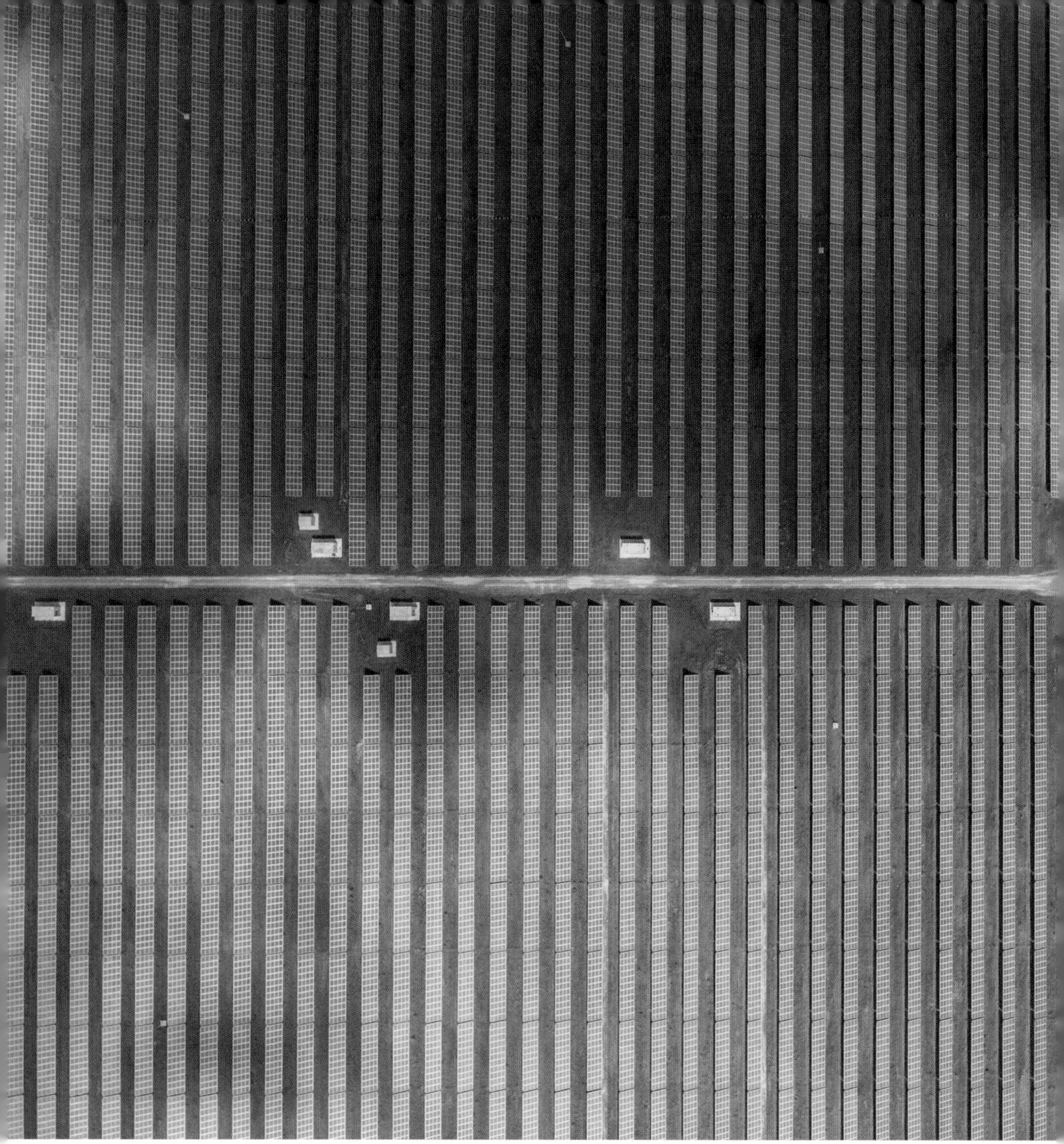

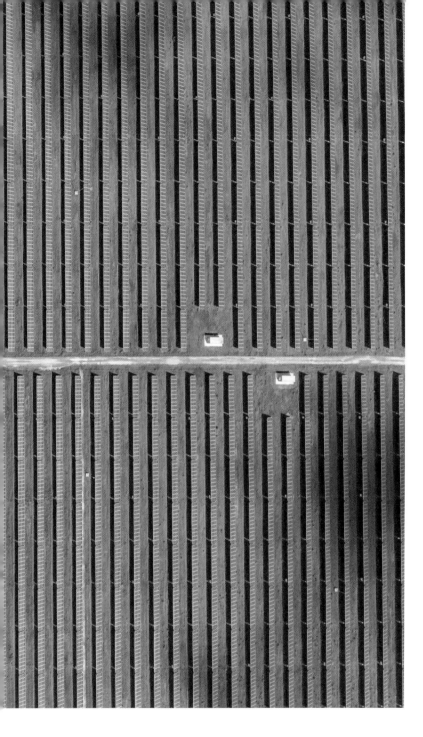

A solar power station near the village Starokozache
occupies 80 hectares.

Sivershchyna

Snovsk. The Tkachenko Brothers

Oleh and Viktor Tkachenko are twin brothers working as mechanics in the locomotive depot in the town of Snovsk. Their depot is one of the only few remaining in Ukraine that carries out specialized repair of steam locomotives.

Oleh and Viktor, together with their younger brother Mykhailo, are members of a small team of mechanics who still have skills for repairing unique models of steam trains, the majority of which have their history started at the end of the 19th century.

Ferries on the Desna River

The Desna is one of the largest rivers in Ukraine. There are many settlements on its banks, but very few ferries that connect them are operating nowadays . There are ferries in Desnianske, Radychiv, and Mezyn villages, and down the river in Sosnytsia and Makoshyne. Also, there are pontoon crossings in Byryne and Maksaky villages.

Ferries are still used daily to get faster to towns, markets, or elsewhere rather than a roundabout route by the road with bridges.

Even if there is only one person willing to cross the river, a ferryman will not refuse to provide a service.

— Well, I'm not as global as the state. The state can neglect couple of hundred of people, but for me, even if there is only one person, I will provide a transport.

The ferry operates daily until the Desna gets frozen. In such a case, a special passage is made for cars, so they can cross the river on ice.

Obyrok

Hamlet Obyrok is an artistic settlement near the town of Bakhmach. It was created by uniting several smaller hamlets: Katsiry, Prokhory, and Koroli. This place, surrounded by pine woods, is ideal for relaxation and art events.

Among the most noteworthy art objects at Obyrok are several Soviet-era monuments with trees growing on. This is a 'Garden of the Empire Decay', where nature unmercifully destroys what used to be considered indestructible.

The hamlet was founded by film director Leonid Kanter, who travelled around the world in 2010 to set kitchen stools on the shores of four oceans: in France, Sri Lanka, Spitsbergen, and on Cape Horn. During this trip, Leonid shot the documentary that became the basis for the movie Human with a Stool.

The Mezyn National Nature Park has a territory of over 31,000 hectares. More than 50 archaeological monuments are preserved here. The most famous one is a Mezyn Paleolithic site. There is a number of historical settlements on the territory of the park and nearby. Architectural monuments include buildings and temples; architectural and park ensembles.

Oleshnia. The Potter Ivan Bibik

Oleshnia village has long been famous for its potters.

— In our village, a girl wouldn't go out with a guy if he didn't have a potter's wheel.

Ivan Bibik, one of the last potters from Oleshnia, told us this. Today, there are just a few of them in the whole village. Ivan's family has been making pottery for generations. Similarly to many other potters from Oleshnia, he learned this craft when he was still a child. Ivan earned his first money for the small plates he made and sold on the market together with his father's handiwork. Visitors from all over Ukraine come to learn pottery skills from Ivan, though his own children chose not to continue family business.

 Mykyta Zavilinskyi   119

Kachanivka is the largest palace and park ensemble in Ukraine from the Classicism period. It was founded in the 1770s as the residence of Count Rumyantsev-Zadunaisky.

The Mizhrichynskyi Park

The Mizhrichynskyi Park is among the largest regional landscape parks in Ukraine. Its area is 100,000 hectares. The territory between the Dnipro and the Desna rivers ('mizhrichchia' in Ukrainian, which gave the name to the park) is one of the most southern terrains that looks like tundra or taiga.

There are moss swamps, moorlands, sand dunes, and glades with sparse trees in the park. Its central part is a forest that protects wildlife. A lynx, which can be found here, is on the emblem of the park.

Yurii Dakhno's Museum in Moskali

In Moskali village, near Chernihiv, there are less than 20 houses remaining. One kilometre long central street has neither a school nor a healthcare facility. However, there is a museum.

A local resident Yurii Dakhno created his own Skansen here: he preserved old houses and a shop that he bought and turned into museums of antiquities. The exhibits include household items of the 19–20th centuries together with artwork from local artists. There are paintings on the walls of the former shop, glass bottles and mugs on the shelves, wooden barrels, straw hats hanging on the pegs, a gramophone, an old radio, and shoes, hiding behind the drawers.

The old house converted into a museum has more furniture: chests, wooden beds, and chairs that were typical for rural life in the 1940s and 1950s.

Yurii bought most of the items from locals, but some exhibits are from craftsmen from other places. The collector says, he knows the origin of almost all of the exhibits.

The museum was not created for profit — visitors are rare here, but sometimes guests from other parts of Ukraine or foreigners stop by. Yurii says that his collection is his creative escape.

The exposition that Yurii has gathered is valuable for ethnography. In 1932, most of the village had burned down, so the clothes and tools that survived became a rarity.

The Blakytni Lakes ('Blue Lakes') in Sivershchyna are quarries filled by water springs and surrounded by pine woods near Oleshnia village. Quartz sand for glass production was extracted here in the past. The biggest of the four lakes is called Velyke ('Big'). Some people also call it Sertse ('Heart') because of its shape.

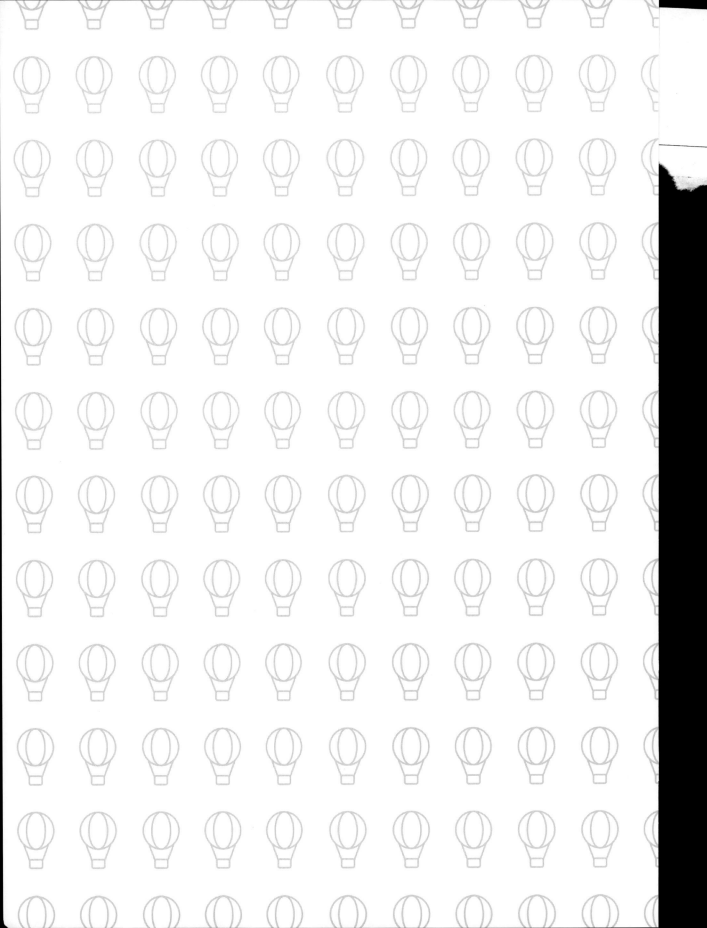

Podillia

the town borders three regions — Podillia, Bukovyna, and Halychyna. Since a railway appeared in the 19th century, this place began to attract more tourists. The resort became popular owing to its climate, which resembles the Mediterranean. Steep slopes of the Dnister canyon around the peninsula do not let the warm air out. To get to Zalishchyky, you need to use either one of two bridges or a ferryboat travelling from the other bank of the Dnister River.

The Broom Republic

Savran, Osychky, and Vilshanka are best known as villages where brooms are made. People call them 'environmentally friendly vacuum cleaners'. Children, teenagers, adults, and elderly people alike deal with broom weaving. For an experienced craftsperson, it takes only five minutes to finish one broom. However, it all depends on the person, his temperament, and pace of work.

To local people, broom weaving means additional income. It is a family tradition that has been passed from generation to generation. People make brooms during the week, and then sell them at the market in Savran, which opens at 7 a.m. on Thursdays. There is less than an hour to buy everything on the list. The market closes within a short time. Brooms can only be bought wholesale. They come in packages, 50 items in each.

Bakota

Bakota, a flooded village not far from Kamianets-Podilskyi, is known for its picturesque landscapes. In 1981, due to the construction of Novodnistrovsk Hydropower Plant, all local residents were forced to move to the nearest towns. Bakota and other villages nearby were flooded. Nowadays, this water reservoir is 200 kilometres long, and the flooded fields stretch over a distance of 1,590 hectares.

Bakota was founded as a town. It was mentioned for the first time in the chronicle of 1240 as the largest administrative centre of Dnister Ponyzzia, with over 3,000 people. In the 13–14th centuries, the area between the Dnister and the Buh rivers was known under the name of Rus Dolna, with the capital in Bakota. It used to be a crossing point of both land and water trade routes.

Motoball

Motoball is a kind of sport played solely in Europe. It originally came from France and became popular in Ukraine during the Soviet period. In Kamianets-Podilskyi, motoball dates back to 1966. A stadium designed specifically for it was built in 1982.

A motoball field resembles a football pitch in terms of dimensions, but the marking is slightly different: there is no circle in the centre, and goalposts have the shape of a semicircle. As for the surface, it is normally covered with asphalt or gravel. To allow for manoeuvring capabilities of motorcycles, asphalt should be dusted with sand. The ball used for this sport is several times larger than the football one. A team consists of five players, including a goalkeeper, each of them on a motorbike.

In Ukraine, a game lasts for four periods, 15 minutes each. In other European countries, game has three periods, 20 minutes each. For one game, eight motorcycles require 40 litres of fuel. The same amount is needed for training.

Malanka Celebration in Osychky

Malanka celebrations in the village of Osychky is authentic, as people managed to preserve their old traditions without meddling tourists or media.

The main characters include Malanka who is played by a boy, between four and seven years old, dressed as a girl; a Cossack, wearing a military outfit of the Soviet times, who accompanies Malanka on her way to every house; singers performing traditional carols — 'koliadkas' — near every house; and Didoks, mythstical figures who act quite wild and scandalous. Their main task is to protect Malanka.

Hot Air Balloons

The long-standing city of Kamianets-Podilskyi is known for its fortress, organic mix of cultures from various nations, and vivid festival life. The most remarkable of those, in particular, is the hot air balloon festival.

As its proponents believe, Kamianets-Podilskyi has every chance to become the centre of aeronautics. It was the terrain suitable for manoeuvres that en- couraged them to found an aeronautics club. Twice a year, the city hosts hot air balloon festivals. At the beginning of May, the season starts with the Podillia Cup festival, followed by Golden Omega festival in October.

— It is like yachting. Although yachts only use one horizontal plane, while we have got an endless number of different planes.

Bukatynka. The Alioshkin museum

Bukatynka is famous for its unique landscapes — there are signs of fossils left from the Earth formation period and volcanic eruptions. This village used to be one of the centres of stone-cutting craft. Maintaining traditions and collecting items of this ancient craft were the main reasons why this artist couple — Oleksii and Liudmyla Alioshkin — settled down in Bukatynka more than 40 years ago. They founded a gallery that exhibits various sculptures, each conveying a unique message. At first, the couple lived in a dugout hut. Then, with their parents' help, they built a two-storey house. When abandoned houses in the neighbourhood came up for sale, the Alioshkins bought them and turned into museums.

Oleksii Karpovych   143

The Fortress of Kamianets-Podilskyi

The fortress of Kamianets-Podilskyi is among the most renowned fortifications in Ukraine. It towers above the rocky headland while the surrounding canyons of the Smotrych River serve as natural barriers. While the first fortifications were built during the times of the Kyivan Rus, it was not until the 15–17th centuries that the fortress began to resemble the site we see today. The indomitable spirit of the medieval outpost leaves a strong impression. Now it is an open-air museum featuring replications of traditional crafts from various historical periods.

From Odesa to Shershentsi

The village of Shershentsi is located in the valley of the river Biloch, bordering with Moldova. Before Dmytro Skoryk and his wife Nadia moved there, they had lived in Odesa for 35 years. Within a few years, they fitted up an ethnic manor house in the village, set up their own brand, and launched the production. The couple host tourists in the 'Bilochi' manor house, where the latter can enjoy home-made dairy products.

The Skoryk family decided to revive their ancestors' traditions. They want to prove it to themselves and everyone else that it is possible to live off the land without relying on someone else's money. Dmytro and Nadia know, preserve, and try to replicate the Ukrainian traditions. It all started on their wedding day, when they dressed in the traditional Ukrainian attire, specific to this region.

— After our wedding in 2008, people in the neighbourhood started to value traditions and incorpo-
rate them into their everyday lives. Our traditions
are something to be proud of. They are priceless.

The unusual aerial view of crop fields.

The Carpathians

The Buddhists from Donetsk

One of the oldest Buddhist communities in Ukraine, originating from Donetsk, resides near the village Kryvopillia. The monks shave their heads and wear white gowns with orange cloaks. They wake up at dawn to read prayers to the sun. They have unconventional appearances and lifestyles compared to other Ukrainians, however, they live in the Carpathians and speak Ukrainian.

The first Buddhist religious community was officially registered in Donetsk in 1991. Before the war with Russia broke out, the activity of Buddhist centres in independent Ukraine had been mostly focused on Slobozhanshchyna region.

Serhii Filonenko, a monk of the Lotus Sutra Order, says that their community was founded right after Ukraine proclaimed its independence, and it was registered with the help of Ukrainian theologist Ihor Kozlovskyi.

Alina Kondratenko   153

Green Construction in Slavske

The architects Eduard Pastukh and Olha Sukha are involved in green construction in the Carpathians. They design energy sustainable houses and are constantly looking for natural construction materials. Nowadays, the most popular materials are straw, hemp, petroleum, and clay.

— Ecology is all about optimized spaces you live in. It is the ability to appreciate the important and to get rid of the unnecessary. It is understanding of what you really need.

The social component of a green project is very important to the couple. In the village of Slavske, they have founded a platform for creative experiments and retreats — Creative Residence MC-6. People come here to experience the viability of green technologies and to have a 'real feel' of green materials.

Ornithopter

An amateur inventor, Volodymyr Yakovenko has been living in the village Iltsi for more than 30 years. He researches, designs, builds, and tests his own ornithopter, a mechanism invented 500 years ago but still not employed completely.

Volodymyr has been mesmerized with the concept of flight for his entire life. At first, he studied theory for a long time. There was no easy access to the Internet back then, so he used to get information from any source he possibly could — he read the Soviet magazines Kryla Batkivshchyny (The Wings of the Motherland) and Tekhnika Molodi (Technology for Youth), spent hours in the library in Ivano-Frankivsk, studied different types of engines, and researched various sources of energy. The ornithopter is his lifetime project, and the inventor has been working on it on his own.

— An ornithopter is a 'tough nut to crack'. It is hard-
er to construct than a delta plane or a car. A car
has more details, that's true, but to have at least a
10-metre flight is way more difficult. The air is an
environment that is more complicated and danger-
ous than the earth. It will not forgive you any mis-
take. That's why it's more challenging.

Alina Kondratenko   157

Polonyna on Sokilskyi Crest

The spouses Vasyl and Maria Petrychuk live and work on Sokilskyi Crest, between the villages Babyn and Yavoriv. During grazing season that lasts for four months, Vasyl takes his herd to polonyna every single day. In summer, villagers entrust their sheep to Vasyl for grazing or milking and making cheese. The couple earns their living this way during warm seasons.In winter, sheep have offspring. During the cold season, the Petrychuks family look after their homestead, and Maria makes 'lizhnyks' (blankets from sheep wool) and woolen footwear for sale.

Cheesemaking does not bring big profits. Despite this, and despite their age, the Petrychuks don't intend to quit sheep breeding.

— Well, we've got used to the fact that we must do it. Young people don't want to engage to this work. They want a lot of money, and there isn't much here. We are pretty old, and we are absolutely fine with the amount we get.

A serpentine on the entry road to the town Turka.

Lizhnyk from Yavoriv

A lizhnyk is a blanket woven from sheep wool. They are traditionally made in the Hutsul village Yavoriv and used in ceremonies and daily life. People use them to cover beds, benches, and carts; they also cover up in lizhnyks in winter.

— The thing we like about our art is its uniqueness — you won't find the same anywhere else in the world.

We are simple people, but we create something that's one-of-a-kind.

Many villagers in Yavoriv have looms at home, which is why locals are involved in lizhnyk making since childhood. The technology is traditional — wool is spun into yarn, then a blanket is woven, then felted, then combed out.

The Carpathian Tram

The Carpathian tram is a mountain narrow-gauge train with a 100-year-old history. It is one of four narrow-gauge train lines with a 750 millimetre rail width. The train route starts in the village Vyhoda and goes through the Carpathians along the river Mizunka. It was built for timber transportation, survived two world wars, and changed a couple of owners. Every weekend, travellers can take a trip and be entertained by a theatrical performance. The train line is a tourist attraction that boosts the development of the town's infrastructure. One can operate a train and watch a movie about its history in the interactive narrow-gauge train museum in Vyhoda.

Pavlo Pashko, Dmytro Bartosh

Polonyna Krynta

Polonyna Krynta (Trans. — 'polonyna' is a Ukrainian word for 'a mountain meadow' in the Carpathians) is famous for Hutsul cheese-making traditions. Today, very few people are involved in this craft. The shepherd who grazes cows is called 'bovhar' at Krynta. Vasyl Kirmoshchuk from the village Verkhovyna became the head of bovhars and started to make cheese when he was 12 years old. Step by step, he turns cattle grazing and cheese making into prof-

itable business. Cattle are gathered from homesteads in nearby villages. As a rule, cattle owners entrust their cows only to bovhars they know personally.

Cheese is made right on the polonyna — the autumn average is 25 kilograms of cheese, and the summer average is 50 kilograms. Salt is the only ingredient added to the cheese.

— Every country and every corner of the world make their own cheese and try to stick to this tradition. Just like we do. People understand that it's tasty, eco-friendly, and without any additives.

Alina Kondratenko, Pavlo Pashko　　167

Christmas in Kryvorivnia

Koliada (Ukrainian traditional carol singing) in the Carpathian village Kryvorivnia is famous for its authenticity and a large number of participants. It lasts for the whole period of Christmas celebrations. Among other Hutsul villages, Kryvorivnia has the biggest number of Koliada batches, or Koliada 'vatahas' (carol singing groups), that consist of people living in different districts of the village. Even the smallest district that includes 20 houses has its own batch.

Every batch is led by a carol singer called 'Bereza' (which means 'a birch' in Ukrainian). It is usually an older man who sets lyrics for each household and the motif of 'plies' (traditional dance pattern for Christmas carols). Carol singers are following this motif rhythmically turning 'bartkas' — traditional Hutsul axes - in their hands .

Oleksandr Khomenko, Dmytro Bartosh   169

Bukovyna

Khotyn Fortress belongs to the list of the oldest fortifications in Ukraine. Rising over the Dnister, it used to protect the water trade route of utmost importance. Even though the stone walls date back to the 13th century, the fortification had been undergoing reconstruction up to the 18th century. 40-metre tall walls of the outpost have withstood multiple attacks over the centuries. However, military assaults would always fail unless the attackers laid a long-lasting siege.

Today, it is a historical and architectural conservation area, which is used as a venue for the Medieval tournaments.

Malanka Celebration in Krasnoyilsk

Malanka, a traditional holiday on St. Basil's day eve or New Year's Day according to the Julian calendar, is authentically celebrated mainly in villages in Bukovyna and Halychyna.

One of the most spectacular events takes place in Krasnoyilsk, the village next to Romania. Every year an unconventional procession draws the attention of a large audience. For two days, all eyes are on the carnival. Locals dress up as animals and mystic and folklore characters. While the design of outfits and masks may vary, the main characters remain the same: a King, a Queen, an Old Man, an Old Woman, a Bear, a Gypsy, a Jew, and Malanka.

Though the name of the carnival originates from the female name Malanka, the procession involves only men. However, as an exception, girls are allowed to

play the characters of Queens and Gypsies during the main celebration, when they make a tour around the houses, accompanied by their small 'Bears' on the morning of January 13.

Costumes of Bears are made of hay or straw, harvested in summer.

Radar Station Pamir

Pamir, an abandoned radar station in Bukovyna, used to be a high-security facility established on Mount Tomnatyk, not far from the Romanian border.

Five antenna cups at 1,565 metres altitude is what remained of airspace surveillance system.

Omnidirectional antennas had been providing continuous monitoring for about 30 years since 1960. Today, this area, intertwined with tourist trails, is popular with travellers as an overnight stop.

Vasyl Salyha, Pavlo Pashko   177

Ionike Semeniuk's Museum
in Hrushivka

Ionike Semeniuk, 80 years old, not only takes care of the large museum of the Moldovan villages Hrushivka and Voloka, but also has energy to race through the village with his former classmate, driving the IZH-49 motorcycle, made in 1951. The villagers cherish the Moldovan traditions and keep them alive.

The village of Voloka is famous for the large-scale production of wedding dresses. In Ionike's museum, you can find old weaver's looms, which were used to make dresses some hundred years ago.

Chernivtsi. Violins by Volodymyr Solodzhuk

The sound of violins made by Volodymyr Solodzhuk is born in a tiny workshop in Chernivtsi. His instruments are winning people's hearts in the concert halls all over the world. At some point, Volodymyr ended his years-long career as a factory engineer in favour of violins that had fascinated him since childhood. The craftsman, who learned on his own, later got a chance to study in Italy. Overall, he has made over 200 musical instruments.

Volodymyr Solodzhuk makes his violins manually. Despite knowing everything and more about structure and operation of musical instruments, Volodymyr does not play any himself. As Volodymyr believes, one can be good at either making instruments or playing them. Wood is an exceptionally important component of high-quality violin sound. Parts of an instrument are made of different types of wood, such as spruce and maple, as each has its unique qualities.

— Why spruce? Because it carries a sound wave faster than any other material. Why maple? Because a backplate made of hard-wooded species retains 27 kilogram cord tension for 300 years. It must be done right, with no frills. Maple carries sound faster than any other hard-wooded types. These two types of wood — maple and spruce — are just what you need.

Chernivtsi National University is a former residence of Bukovynian and Dalmatian Metropolitans. The red-brick building with towers and stone carvings was built in the 19th century. It is a mix of Roman and Byzantine style with gothic, Moresque, and other motifs. The architectural complex includes three buildings — a Metropolitan residence, a Seminary, and a Monastery.

Monuments are embellished with mouldings, carved cornices, and tiles of five different colours. Chernivtsi National University is a popular sightseeing attraction and is a part of the UNESCO World Heritage.

Malanka Celebration in Vashkivtsi

On January 13 and 14, the village of Vashkivtsi in the Bukovyna region turns into a venue for the traditional theatrical celebration of Malanka, also known among locals as 'Pereberia', which means 'a costume party'. Since the end of the 19th century, when villagers started to dress up in costumes and masks, the Malanka celebration in Vashkivtsi has become an outstanding carnival.

Traditional dressing up for Malanka used to be forbidden by both the Romanian and the Soviet governments. Nevertheless, after the Second World War, villagers still proceeded with celebrations, breaking the Soviet laws. Up till today, Malanka has remained a splendid occasion, hugely popular with tourists.

In Vashkivtsi, common characters of Malanka fes-
tivities include a Cossack, a Police Officer, an Uhlan
(a cavalryman), an Old Man, an Old Woman, a Bear,
a Gypsy, and a Jew. Malanka is played by a guy
dressed as a girl in traditional Bukovynian attire.
Another female character is a Ukrainian, which may
be played by girls. However, the main symbol of this
holiday is a Goat.

Tavria

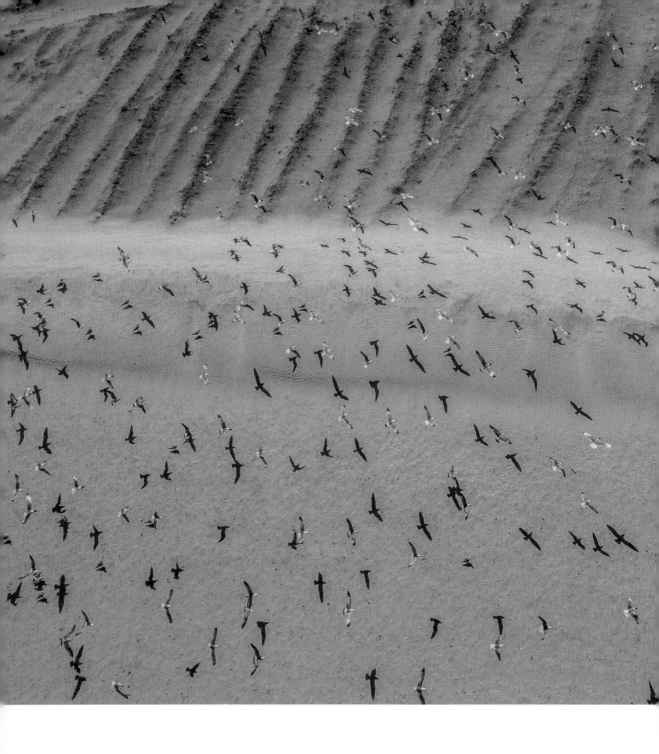

Birds are flying over the dunes of a semi-desert in Tavria, near the Kinburn spit.

Adzyhol Lighthouse

The Adzyhol Lighthouse in the middle of the Dnipro estuary, is the tallest lighthouse in Ukraine. It was built upon engineer Shukhov's design in 1911. Thousands of studs hold together beams to compose a 64-metre skeletal steel building. Such a design allowed to make the building not only lighter, but also resilient against the storms of any volume. The lighthouse has lived through the wars and still works today. It offers a marvellous view on the Kinburn spit, Stanislav slopes, and Rybalche village.

Yurii Stephanyak, Pavlo Pashko   191

Buhai. Ukrainian tailed drum

Buhai is one of the rare and extraordinary folk instruments. It attracted a lot of attention when ONUKA, Ukrainian electro-folk band, has used it on stage, while performing intermediate act during the Eurovision Song Contest, which was held in Kyiv in 2017. Andrii Lopushynskyi got into making buhais way earlier. Andrii's previous experience in making percussions for historic reconstruction clubs paid off largely when making his first buhai.

Buhai is a cord and friction percussion musical instrument, where the sound is produced by a finger friction against its membrane or horse-hair bundle fixed in its centre. One plays buhai with moistened fingers by pulling the bundle with a slipping motion. The pitch of the sound depends on where fingers stop on the bundle.

In Ukraine, buhai is usually an accompanying ensemble instrument. Along with folk bands, carol singing batches play it for musical accompaniment.

— Buhai is officially recognized Ukrainian folk instrument, however people don't recognize it when they see it for the first time, mistaking it for an African instrument.

Alina Kondratenko   193

A nesting spot of white egrets on the Kinburn spit. The great egret lives separately from other birds and is very protective against representatives of its own kind. They feed in flocks.

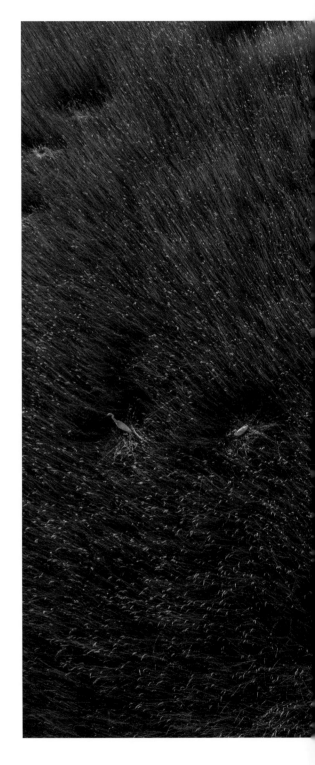

Kherson Reed Beds

Kherson is located on the right bank of the Dnipro River, in the south of Ukraine. It entered history as the city of ships and sailors, the place where the Black Sea Navy Fleet was born. Today, it is a rather big seaport and river port on Dnipro. Water is an integral part of the city life. It is a landmark, a major recreation place, a helper in work, and the best friend for children and adults. One can travel around by water taxi. When it's a mushroom season, people sail a yacht to pick them. The Kherson family of Shyshka and Blummer work with young yacht enthusiasts — father, mother, and two daughters are coaches in yachting school on one of the Kherson islands.

Velyki Kopani and Cabbages

In the village Velyki Kopani, near Kherson, you can hardly find a household not growing vegetables for sale. One of the biggest wholesale vegetable markets — 'Nezhdanyi' — is located here.

— Everyone works in the field. It's not a hobby — it's a lifestyle. It's warm here, and there is plenty of water. We are in the south. Since there is no industry here, people have no other place to work. We do our best to earn our living.

One of the market's peculiarities is early-season fruits and vegetables. The prices at 'Nezhdanyi' market influence the prices of fruits, vegetables, and berries in all regions of Ukraine since prices in Velyki Kopani set up the starting point for all shopping centres, distributors, and processing companies.

Mykyta Zavilinskyi, Pavlo Pashko   199

Stone-Carved Vyshyvankas

Nova Kakhovka is a young town founded in the 1950s as a residential cluster for hydroelectric complex construction workers. All buildings here were built hastily in accordance with standard construction project, thus turned out dull and blank. Hryhorii Dovzhenko, an artist and a follower of Boichukism style (named after Mykhailo Boichuk, a Ukrainian monumental painter), arrived in Nova Kakhovka during that time. In collaboration with his colleagues, he created 80 unique carved panels that decorated the walls of all buildings and changed the face of the city. Very shortly, the Soviet media criticized Dovzhenko for his 'architectural redundancies'. Nowadays, his creations are considered to be a unique art object called 'stone-carved vyshyvankas'(traditional embroideries).

— People recall how visitors coming to Nova Kakhovka were impressed with whitewashed houses, flourishing trees and flowers, and the ornaments sparkling in the sun. The patterns on backgrounds with various brightness and color — violet, green, lilac — were made by artists to look like white waving. Many said that the town looked as if garnished with laces.

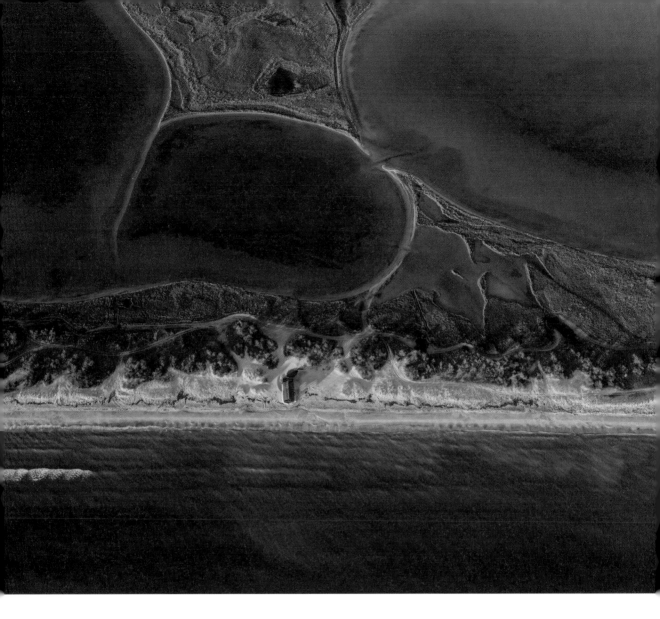

The Kinburn Spit

Kinburn spit separates Dnipro-Buh estuary from the Black Sea. It is washed by fresh and salty waters that even differ in colour. The 40-metre sand spit is an extension of the Kinburn peninsula. On its very edge, the sea and the estuary are just a few meters apart. It is a favourite nesting place and an intermittent spot for birds during their migration. Even an artificial peninsula was created for birds next to Lopushne lake.

Salt Lakes

Near the village Heroiske, the salt extraction is carried out in an old way, by gradual evaporation. The method presupposes sea water being moved through a cascade of salt pans. Salt concentration increases by 27 per cent under the sun, and the crystallization starts.

This production process has been preserved since 1898. However, way before that the Cossacks (independent military units, emerged in XV century) used salt from this place. The ponds vary in color depending on concentration of beta-carotene and magnesium in water.

Prychornomoria

40-metre loamy cliffs stand high in the steppe
shores of Dnipro-Buh estuary.

Olbia

Olbia is a complex of historical monuments of an ancient polis in Prychornomoria founded as a Greek colony in the 600s B.C. Today, it is the National Historical and Archaeological Reserve and Museum with artefacts of the ancient culture, including sarcophagi, various household bowls, and plates. The territory of the reserve includes a settlement and a necropolis. Berezan Island, where the oldest Ancient Greek settlement in the Northern Prychornomoria was located, is also a part of the reserve.

With only about 17,000 visitors per year, this unique place near the city of Mykolaiv can be considered an unknown destination.

Pavlo Pashko   211

Bakhtov Family House

Volodymyr Bakhtov has been fascinated by the cities of Ancient Greece since childhood. He fulfilled his dream to travel on a bireme — a wooden ship restored with maximum resemblance to ancient vessels. This trip inspired him to move to one of such ancient cities, Olbia, where together with his wife he has built a house-workshop, using ancient Greek plans. Bakhtov's house is situated some hundred meters from Olbia, in Parutyne village. It is not only a workshop for artists, but also a museum and a gallery. Volodymyr and Tetiana reconsider Ancient Greece and create modern artworks using ancient techniques, visual images, and even broken pieces of clay dishes that were found in ancient Olbia.

Field on the territory of Tylihul Nature Reserve near the village Kobleve.

Odesa Astronomical Observatory

Odesa Astronomical Observatory was the main astronomical observatory of Ukraine during the Soviet times. It was built in 1871; at that time there were no park or city nearby. The conditions were perfect for observing space. However, the lights of coastal city Odesa today hinder normal research work here, even with all facilities in place. Most observations are now carried out at Maiaky station, 40 kilometres away from Odesa.

Aktove Canyon

Aktove Canyon is more than 50 metres deep gap in the bare steppe formed by the river Mertvovod in granite rocks near the village Aktove.

Navigable up until the 20th century, Mertvovod river is shallow and silty today. Dams constructed during the Soviet times significantly declined water level. The canyon is a part of the National Nature Park 'Buzkyi Hard'.

The sunrise at Prymorskyi Boulevard in Odesa.

Pavlo Pashko, Yurii Stephanyak

Buzkyi Hard National Nature Park

The National Nature Park includes protected areas and geological monuments. With its rocky river canyons and numerous rapids in waters, this place stands out from the steppe areas around.

The cascade of rapids on the river Southern Buh near the village Myhiia attracts those eager for rafting. The kayaking route is the second most difficult in Ukraine, and is used for international rafting competitions.

A tractor is ploughing a field near the modern nut-tree farm in Troitske village.

Pavlo Pashko   225

Podniprovia
and Zaporizhzhia

A view of the riverfront of Dnipro city from Monastyrskii Island.

Khortytsia

Khortytsia is the largest island on Dnipro, down the river from the Dnipro Hydroelectric Station in Zaporizhzhia. This is where Ukrainian history comes to life.

Khortytsia has been long known because of Dnipro rapids — rock formations rising in the stream of Dnipro river between the modern cities Dnipro and Zaporizhzhia.

But almost a century ago, concrete dams of the Dnipro Hydroelectric Station raised the water level by 40 metres, and the rapids disappeared under the water — the river became navigable.

Today, the historical complex 'Zaporizhian Sich', which represents a generalized image of the Cossack Sich (fortification), is located on Khortytsia.

Petrykivka Painting

Petrykivka is a traditional painting style that formed in the village Petrykivka; however, it was spread throughout a larger territory. Petrykivka painting is believed to originate from the tradition to draw on external house walls in villages.

The oldest examples of paintings, which were preserved by historians, date back to the beginning of the 20th century. In the 1930s, a school of decorative painting, where a whole generation of artisans studied, was opened in Petrykivka. This is how Petrykivka painting transformed from folk art to modern art.

In 2003, Petrykivka painting was inscribed on the Representative List of the Intangible Cultural Heritage of Humanity by UNESCO.

— Rhythm is a basis for the composition. Green leaves, blue vines, buds, flowers — all of them should be placed rhythmically. This rhythm is nothing but a reflection of life cycles, nature, and space.

Dnipro. The potter Serhii Horban

Serhii Horban has his pottery workshop close to the city centre of Dnipro. Serhii was born in Dnipro, and never studied pottery. He says that he learned a lot from books and the Internet. The first time he met a real potter was in Opishne village, Poltava region, famous for its pottery traditions. Serhii got his first piece of clay as a present from his friend who took up to making ceramics earlier and used to cast ware in plaster moulds. Serhii always wanted to work with a potter's wheel — now he teaches pottery in his workshop.

Birds inhabit protected islands in the middle of Zaporizhzhia, near the Dnipro Hydroelectric Station and Khortytsia Reserve.

Dobropasove. The Cucumber Cluster

Dobropasove may be called a cucumber cluster.
Every second household in this village has been
growing vegetables, particularly cucumbers, for
generations.

Naddniprianshchyna

Rock canyon, formed in Proterozoic granites, at the river Hirskyi Tikych near the village Buky.

Makariv. The Inventor Volodymyr Vavilov

Volodymyr Vavilov is a self-taught craftsman from the town Makariv. He has created a fantastic car with his own hands. Volodymyr bought an old Fiat for about 150 USD, and then invested more than 10,000 USD in tuning. The six-wheeled car resembles a spaceship with a figure of an Alien — a character from the movie with the same name — that sits comfortably on the roof. This wonder car has eight exhaust pipes, wheels with backlighting, and several TVs inside.

— The aim was to make a car that would impress. I think I have achieved that already. I would never afford a nice car, but I can make one myself.

The Roma of Zolotonosha

Zolotonosha population of 30,000 people includes 2,000 Roma. They founded two NGOs — Cherkasy regional NGO 'Romani Rota' and Zolotonosha Gypsy Commune 'Ame Roma'. Centre 'Dialogue Between Generations', which is one of a kind in Ukraine, is where the Roma people can get medical assistance, have a rest, do laundry, take a shower. The Roma of Zolotonosha are mostly engaged in trade and private entrepreneurship. There are no nomadic Roma in Zolotonosha, however some number of internally displaced people are living disorderly and sometimes without proper hygiene conditions.

Thanks to local activists, the Roma people have the opportunity to go to the same schools, churches, shops, and markets as other residents. They are active participants of city and regional events; however, they still remain not fully integrated into society.

— The aim is to integrate the Roma into Ukrainian
society. I consider myself Ukrainian of Roma origin,
and I'd like the others to do the same. For example,
Ukrainians from Western and Eastern Ukraine are
still Ukrainians. We need to build our state and our
home and not be fooled by any provocations.

Alina Kondratenko   247

Revivka dam between Svitlovodsk city and
Podorozhnie village.

Goat Farms

From the beginning of the 2000s, goat farms began to emerge and develop in Ukraine. Previously, this type of farming was totally unpopular — in the Soviet Union, a goat was considered a non-profitable animal. During the expedition to Naddniprianshchyna, we were lucky to visit four goat farms: 'Zolota Koza' (Golden Goat), 'Babyni Kozy' (Grandma's Goats), 'Lisova Ferma' (Forest Farm), and 'Pani Koza' (Mrs. Goat). There is a lot of information on the benefits of goat milk today, so the demand for goat-milk products has increased in city stores.

Guitars from Bila Tserkva

Universum Guitars is a guitar factory founded in Bila Tserkva in 2016. Guitars are made in serial production, following recommendations of musicians.

The first guitar that has been designed here has both acoustic and electroacoustic modes. Designer Oleksandr Doroshenko says this is the musical know-how of Ukrainians.

— Nobody in the world had been doing it before we did. We were the first to put a condenser microphone inside the box-frame instrument. There is a mix between the microphone and the sensor — that is what electroacoustic mode means.

The Dakhovskis' Mansion

The Dakhovskis' mansion is yet an unacknowledged unique architectural monument built in Leskove village in the 19th century. Legend says, the palace was built to outdo Count Potocki, who established 'Sofiivka' landscape park in Uman town. The landlords Dakhovskyi decided to build a palace styled as English Medieval castle. The palace constructed in the 1850s impresses with its scale and scope.

In the Soviet times, the mansion was given to the Soviet military, and acquired the status of regime object. Its location was undisclosed.

Both back then and today, high artistic value of the estate was not duly considered. During the Soviet times, the palace also served as a camp for pioneers (scout-like organization for youth in the USSR), a military hospital, and a warehouse for medicines.

The estate still belongs to the Ministry of Defense of Ukraine — access is possible only with the permission from military unit commander.

Zernoland in Ivkivtsi

An open-air museum of bread making is situated in Ivkivtsi village. Nazar Lavrinenko, together with his team, restored an authentic mill there. Visitors of Zernoland are involved in all stages of bread making. The complex has its own smithy, pottery, ethnographic museum, and area with table games of the Haidamakas' (cossac paramilitary groups, fighting against Polish-Lithuanian rule in the 18th century) times.

Volyn

The green tunnel is stretching over the railway between villages Klevan and Orzhiv. This place is widely popular with Japanese people thanks to movie director Akiyoshi Imazeki, who produced the romantic drama Tunnel of Love: The Place for Miracles in 2014.

The Luge Track in Kremenets

The Ukrainian Summer Luge Championship takes place at Ukraine's only wooden luge track in Kremenets town. It was not until the mid-1990s that the reconstruction of the 1,157-metres-long luge track began, even though the first track had been built back in the 19th century. The luge track belongs to the sports training base that hosts international sleigh and roller skates race competition every year.

The first ski-jump ramps and pistes built in the vicinity of Kremenets started inception of winter sports in this region in the 1930s. It is now used as a training base for professional athletes. However, from April to October, tourists also may go for a spin at the less challenging part of the track.

Tarakaniv Fort

The remains of the unique military facility of the late 19th century. The fort is situated next to Dubno town, not far from the village of Tarakaniv. Oddly enough, the facility is still assigned to the armed forces, even though it has been long since it was last used for military purposes.

The fort's design is attributed to the German military engineer Eduard Totleben, who acted on the order of the Russian Empire. The fort marked the border between Russian and Austro-Hungarian Empires after the Third Partition of Poland.

From the 1870s to the 1880s, the fort was built at quite a fast pace. Modernization of constructions, which lasted until 1908, introduced a new material for building — concrete — in addition to stones and bricks.

The fort is diamond-shaped, up to 240 metres wide on each side. On the outside, it is surrounded with a deep trench and earth mounds, reinforced with thick walls. In the centre, there are two-storey barracks that can be accessed through four underground passages under the second earth mound.

Lubart's castle, the Upper castle of Lutsk, is one of two partly preserved castles and one of the oldest buildings of the region.

Ostroh Academy

Ostroh Academy, the first-ever university in Eastern Europe, was founded by Prince Kostyantyn of Ostroh in 1576. A year before, he had established a printing house here and invited Ivan Fedorovych (inventor of the printing press) to develop it. After the prince's death, the academy eventually fell into decay. The same fate befell the town of Ostroh. Under the Soviet rule, the town acquired a reputation for its mental health clinic where 'rebellious' academics and intellectuals were restrained.

In the early 1990s, idea to revive the university in Ostroh appeared. Ihor Pasichnyk was assigned its principal, and he began with recruiting young

people who were not afraid to start a university from scratch meeting the world quality standards. Applicants were supposed to meet strict selection criteria, such as English language proficiency, willingness to do an internship abroad, profound knowledge, teaching skills, and young age.

— I am interested in shaping a community of Ukrainian intellectuals, young people who would not seek a better life abroad. But even if they do, I want them to work in the field matching their degree.

Fisherman's hut in the village of Staryi Solotvyn amid the Kodnianka river. Once an abandoned hut surrounded by water, now – a small island, which has become a popular tourist destination.

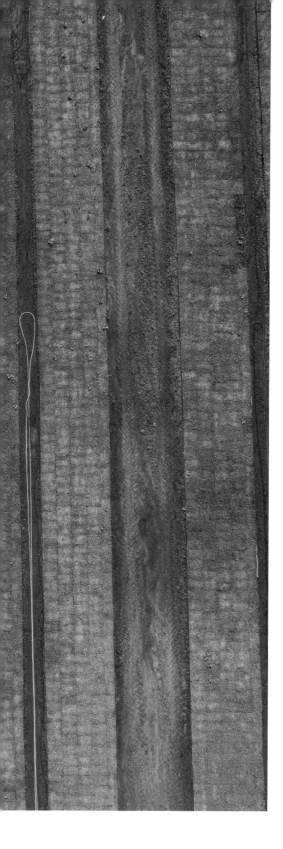

Chinese Cabbage Pool in Khorokhoryn

Owing to some entrepreneurs, the village of Khorokhoryn has turned into a pool of growing strawberries and Chinese cabbage. There is not a single household that is not occupied with farming or engaged in supply chain.

It all started after some villagers went to Poland for seasonal labour and came back with Chinese cabbage seeds. They followed the example of Polish farmer for whom they had been working for some years and started to grow the cabbage at home. Back in those days, over half of the households were abandoned because their owners used to earn their living in Poland. However, as cabbage growing turned out successful, it inspired the others. No one considers seasonal labour abroad as an option now. Cabbage and strawberries grown in Khorokhoryn are sold across Ukraine and exported to Belarus.

Slobozhanshchyna

The House 'Slovo'

'Slovo' ('word' in Ukrainian), a residential building in Kharkiv, has become a symbol of the Soviet purge against intellectuals. It used to be a writers' housing cooperative. Its former residents are now considered canonical writers of Ukrainian literature. In 1930s, most of them were persecuted and later executed. The building is still residential.

Derzhprom. The House of State Industry

Thirteen-storey Derzhprom was the first skyscraper in the USSR. This monument, designed in constructivism style, is situated at Svobody square, which is the largest in Ukraine. The building boasts both aesthetic and functional facets. Its construction has been considered a breakthrough. Back in the days of the Ukrainian Soviet Socialist Republic, Kharkiv needed such building to maintain the status of the capital. Construction was stopped twice due to the lack of funding. However, five years after Derzhprom had been built in Kharkiv, the status of capital returned to Kyiv.

Air Patrol

The community organization Civil Air Patrol was established in Kharkiv after the Maidan revolution in 2014 and Russian military assault against Ukraine. Ever since then, Civil Air Patrol has saved countless lives and provided assistance in protecting Ukrainian borders. This is a community of qualified pilots who do their job voluntarily with private aircraft. Yurii Pokusai, the head of the organization, believes that personal efforts are enough to change the country for better.

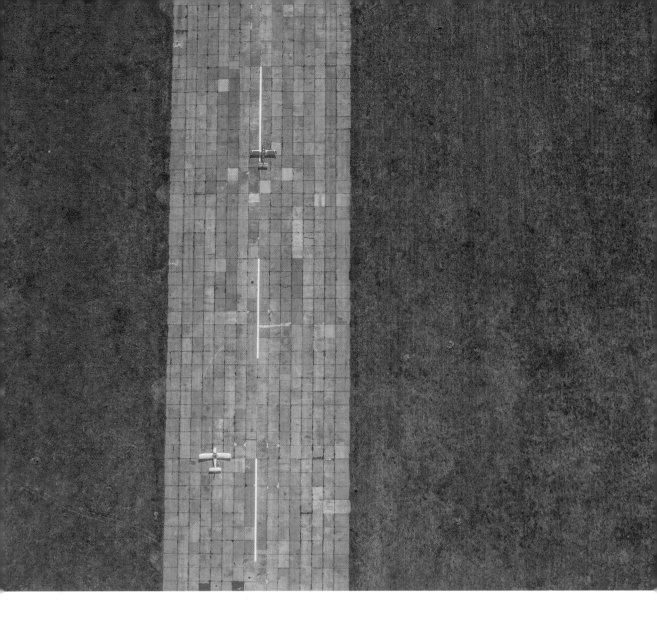

Besides patrolling, they provide training for cadets in Kharkiv. Members of the civil patrol see them-selves as successors to the aviation of the Ukrainian People's Republic, which fought against the Russian Bolshevik army, effectively fulfilling military tasks at the beginning of the 20th century.

Pavlo Pashko, Serhii Sverdelov 281

The view of UTR-2, the largest telescope in the world, located in the vicinity of Chuhuyiv town in Slobozhanshchyna. It is worth noting that the area of this radio telescope is larger than the total area of all telescopes of the same type in the world.

The Meskhetian Turks

The Meskhetian Turks are a nation scattered around the world. The roots of ethnic Turks go back to the territory known today as Georgia, Meskheti in particular. The Meskhetian Turks are one of the USSR nations that were exposed to repression and expelled from the Caucasus on Stalin's order in 1944. All Meskhetian Turks were expelled from Georgia to Kazakhstan, Uzbekistan, and Azerbaijan. In 1989, after Fergan Pogroms of Uzbeks which resulted in a hundred casualties and more than 700 burned homes, the Meskhetian Turks started emigrating in pursuit of new places to live. That is how they ended up in Ukraine.

This photo was taken in the village of Vasiukivka, some kilometres away from demarcation line from the territory controlled by the 'DNR' terrorist organization.

Potters of Sloviansk

Sloviansk has been long known for its ceramic ware made in tiny pottery workshops, the number of which reaches several hundred. For years, these workshops had been making souvenirs for resort towns, businesses, and large companies. In the course of the occupation of Sloviansk by the 'DNR' terrorist organization, some pottery workshops have been ransacked and required reconstruction.

For many, it became a turning point that made them reconsider their target customers and opt for Western Ukraine instead of Crimea, Donetsk, and Luhansk. Potters in Sloviansk are concerned about the future of their region, which is why they donate their income to support the Ukrainian army.

The Goryuns

Goryun is the name of indigenous people of Putyvl district, the sub-ethnicity that originated in this area in the 16th century. Lukeriia Kosheleva, a Goryun by origin, meets a fellow villager outside her house in the village of Nova Sloboda, Slobozhanshchyna.

The dialect of the Goryun is gradually disappearing, but it can still be heard among the locals. Their language includes Ukrainian, Russian, and Belorussian words. According to one theory, the name Goryun was used to designate people in mourning; while another one suggests that this name occurred because people settled in the areas of burned forests.

Halychyna

Olesko Castle

Olesko Castle, the oldest castle of Halychyna, is an architectural monument of the 13–18th centuries. The location of the castle on the border of Lithuania and Poland led to continuous struggle for the ownership of the place and frequent change of owners. The first time it was mentioned in historical sources was in 1327.

Olesko Castle is famous in Polish history as a place where a grandson of Jan Danilowicz, the future king of Poland Jan III Sobieski, was born in 1629. During his reign, the castle got a status of the royal residence. For the Soviet period, it was turned into a POW camp and a military warehouse. Only in the 1970s active renovation started in Olesko castle.

Emmaus-Oselya

The mutual aid community 'Emmaus-Oselya' is a non-governmental organization with a mission to help homeless people regain their dignity in the community and readapt in society. The community, in turn, learns to accept each person and spreads the ideas of 'Emmaus'.

First of all, 'Emmaus-Oselya' helps homeless people and those in difficult situations. Its aim is to facilitate

people's return to social life by providing them with a manageable amount of workload and accommodation. Everyone works on a daily basis in 'Oselya'; common funds are equally distributed among everyone and spent on common needs. Since the organization has no external funding, it functions solely on the money it makes.

Domazhyr

Domazhyr is a bear shelter near Lviv. Animals that had been kept at hunting training centers, travelling zoos, and circuses in horrible conditions for a long time go through rehabilitation in the shelter.

The rescued animals learn to live in a semi-forest environment inside spacious enclosures. Some bears experience walking on the ground for the first time ever, while the others re-develop their natu-ral skills. After living in captivity, bears can't return into the wild for good.

— It is great to know that we are not alone — more shelters mean more opportunities to solve the problem. Human interference in nature is destructive. The sooner people realize it, the better the chances to increase population of wild animals in natural habitat.

Lyres by Hordii Starukh

Lviv sculptor and musician Hordii Starukh has set himself a goal to learn building hurdy-gurdies and to make 300 of them. This number is not random — there is information that the Soviet authorities had organized a convention for musicians that played 'kobza' (Ukrainian folk musical instrument of the lute family) in the 1930s, and then murdered all 300 participants. In 2009, Hordii Starukh produced his first lyre. Since then he has made dozens, and the geography of customers reaches South Korea.

The craftsman has learned the craft on his own and continues to master his technique and the instruments to make them sound exceptional. Hordii makes the keys and the sounding boards manually. He attaches his original handle that is spiral shaped,

unlike the traditional European S-shaped one. Each lyre is one of a kind and has a unique sound.

Over the years of the Soviet regime, the lyre-making craft decayed, but Hordii is now re-establishing it. The craftsman says that even though he relies on traditions, he makes modern instruments.

— I have a dream to make at least 300 lyres. The history surrounding this art, with the execution of our bards, is a sad one. I will never be able to completely restore the craft of lyre manufacturing, but I will at least do what I can to contribute to its revival and continue it. If I manage to make 300 lyres, my mission will be complete.

!FESTrepublic

One of the most famous transformed industrial environments in Lviv is !FESTrepublic, which provides offices, modern production areas, and free zones for visitors. It was created by Lviv Holding of Emotions !FEST, founded by entrepreneurs Andrii Khudo, Yurii Nazaruk, and Dmytro Herasimov in 2007. In 2015, they purchased an abandoned factory premises 'Halychsklo' (The Halychyna Glass) located in the industrial district Pidzamche. The factory used to produce glass containers for the pharmaceutical industry but after bankruptcy remained vacant for about 10 years. In autumn 2016, !FESTrebulic Club, a place of discos and parties, opened at the premises. In summer 2018, !FEST Coffee Mission Hub also opened its doors.

In 2010, the Holding of Emotions !FEST became partners with the publishing house 'Vydavnytstvo Staroho Leva' (The Old Lion Publishing House). The publishing house headquarters is located on the territory of the !FESTrepublic in a building that looks like a huge bookshelf.

Vytynankas by Dariia Alyoshkina

'Vytynanka' (paper-cutting art) appeared on the territory of Ukraine as a decoration of rural houses in the middle of the 19th century. The art of vytynanka was considered extinct for a while, though a craftswoman from Lviv has discovered a new way to attract attention to this Ukrainian craft by creating vytynankas for modern interiors, public places, and book covers. Dariia creates large-sized vytynanka curtains that have already conquered customers in Poland, France, and even South Korea.

— I started making big format vytynankas and managed to draw attention to them with a 'wow' effect. Later on, people started learning what vytynanka is about and that we have a tradition like this because vytynanka art was considered extinct back in 2008.

Sunset on Parashka mountain

Sunset on Parashka (Paraska) mountain, the highest peak of the range in Skole Beskydy, the Carpathians. The mountain is 1268.5 metres above sea level.

The Swiss Farm in Potutory

In 2007, a Swiss woman, Cristina Lieberherr, arrived to live and work in the village Potutory, near Berezhany. She organized an enterprise that grows ecologically clean tea and herbs.

Cristina came to Ukraine to represent an investor from the organization that encourages small farmers to implement an organic method of farming. She had some experience and recipes of herbal mixes that

she decided to use at her own enterprise. During the first year, Cristina Lieberherr did everything herself and today she has several full-time employees.

They grow Ukrainian dill at the farm, which is considered to be a rare valuable plant in Switzerland. They also grow sage, chamomile, mint, and giant hyssop. Volunteers and tourists are welcome in the farm.

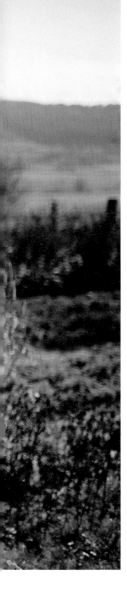

— Everyone who visits Berezhany area admires our hills and forests. During the Austro-Hungarian Empire times, this area was called 'small Switzerland'. Swiss came here, fell in love with the place, and decided to implement a project aimed at development and support of biodynamic agricultural management in Ukraine.

The Ranch 'Skarbova Hora'

In the village Lopushna near Lviv, Ostap Lun has founded a ranch called 'Skarbova Hora' ('Treasure Mountain'). His love for horses inspired him to start socially beneficial community which includes a hippotherapy centre operating since 2010.

Since childhood, Ostap had dreamt about horse riding but he managed to make his dream come true only as an adult. He owns a garment manufactur-

ing business in Lviv that gives him the opportunity and resources to upkeep the ranch.

— I am happy with my lifestyle. Everything here is real. I simply notice this power of nature that is delicate and strong at the same time.

Interaction with horses has physical and emotional benefits. Hippotherapy has a positive effect on

children with disabilities. A horse has to be trained every day for four years to get ready to work with children.

Ostap has developed special language of communication with horses. It mostly comprises of body language because horses mostly react to gestures and body posture.

Kateryna Akvarelna, Khrystyna Kulakovska 309

The Doors to Be Preserved

'Frankivsk that has to be preserved' is the name of a civil movement in Ivano-Frankivsk that has been founded with an aim to preserve historic heritage. It was founded by activist Mariia Kozakevych in 2016 in order to take care of the old entrance doors to historic buildings of Ivano-Frankivsk.

Over a couple of years, the movement succeeded to assemble a team of carpenters, blacksmiths, and stained-glass designers who are involved in restoration as well as the activists who spread the idea. In a short time, they managed to save about 20 doors that were found in garbage disposals and returned to their original places instead of the new plastic ones.

— The name of our organization reflects the state of things in the city — it really needs to be cared for.

Ivano-Frankivsk is a relatively young city and still carries memories of its founders — the Potocki family — as well as recollections of the Austro-Hungarian and West Ukrainian People's Republic periods. Every epoch left some marks on the face of the city: exquisitely embellished mansions, the foundations of Bastion (Stanislav fortress, the 17–19th centuries), churches, and residential houses. The doors and windows were made out of high-quality timber due to the proximity to the Carpathian forests.

Questions and Answers

What is Ukraïner?

Ukraïner is a volunteer multimedia project launched in 2016. We discover Ukraine and turn these discoveries into useful visual content which is already being used in education, as a presentation of regions inside the country as well as to display the touristic potential of Ukraine in the world.

Why is the project called Ukraïner?

The title was born as a result of combining two words expressing the main idea of the project: "Ukraine" and "insider", as we show Ukraine to both Ukrainians and the world from the insiders position. This is how Ukraïner got its name.

How did we gather information for this book?

This book is based on over a dozen research and documentary expeditions, 100,000 kilometres travelled, and more than 400 settlements visited, during which we were looking for answers to the questions 'What is Ukraine really about?' and 'Who are we?' The result is hundreds of video stories, texts, and photos, some of which you can find in this book.

How do we divide Ukraine by regions?

The book has 16 chapters. Each chapter covers one historical region of Ukraine, based on historical and ethnographic borders at the beginning of the XX century. After the World War II, the current region borders have been established letting the Soviet authorities execute their power more efficiently. We aim at unifying the country, therefore we use historical division instead of the one established by the Soviet Union.

Why do we write toponyms in this way?

The League of Nations, the United Nations and other international organizations started the process of unification of toponyms, transliterating them in accordance with the single international standard, in the XX century. During the process of the transliteration standards development, Ukraine was the part of the Soviet Union, therefore had no say in the international arena. All international documents concerning the Soviet Ukraine used toponyms in transliteration from the Russian language - the official language of the Soviet Union - despite their Ukrainian origin. Results of this transliteration policy can be seen in Ukraine and the world even today. Glaring example: Ukraine's capital is still referred to as "Kiev" (transliteration from Russian) instead of "Kyiv" (transliteration from Ukrainian). In this book and in all other materials of Ukraïner we use transliteration of Ukrainian toponyms from the Ukrainian language, in order to change the situation.

How many volunteers are involved in the project?
Now it is more than 300 volunteers who joined the project: authors, photographers, videographers, transcriptionists, subtitlers, editors, proofreaders, producers, translators, coordinators, designers, illustrators, IT specialists, communicators, event organizers, expert advisers, facilitators, layout designers, etc.

Who supports us?
Today, the main source of support is donations. During the lifetime of the project, we were also granted trust by Raiffeisen Bank Aval, a tourist company "Kiy Avia", an automobile brand Land Rover, a mineral water company "Morshynska", a chain of gas stations "OKKO", "!FEST" Holding of Emotions, YedynkaDGTL, Depositphotos, etc.

If you feel the project is doing the right thing, you have a chance to support it and influence its further development. Any contribution to Ukraïner is your contribution to Ukraine!

Support Ukraïner

How to pronounce the names of regions and why these names?

Zakarpattia [zɐkɐrˈpatʲːɐ]
Commonly used name — Transcarpathia.
Western region separated from the rest of the territory of the country by the Carpathian mountains, situated behind (Ukrainian: за, "za") these mountains — The Carpathians.

Pryazovia [prɪɑˈzɔːwʲɐ]
Commonly used name — The Azov Sea Region.
Region washed by the Azov sea in the South, meaning situated by (Ukrainian: при, "pry") the Azov sea.

Poltavshchyna [pʊˈltɑːɥ ʃtʃɪnɐ]
Commonly used name — The Poltava Region.
Region at the left bank of the Dnipro river, between the Naddniprianshchyna to the West and the Slobozhanshchyna to the East. The name of the region derives from the name of the river Ltava.

Polissia [pʊˈlisʲːɐ]
Region at the North-West of the country, covered with forests, as if hidden behind (Ukrainian: по, "po") the forest (Ukrainian: ліс, "lis").

Bessarabia [bɪsːɐˈraːbʲɐ]
Region at the South-West, situated between the Prut and the Dnister rivers, mouth of the Danube river and the Black sea. It is also called Budzhak (Turkish: Bucak — corner). This region was called by Osman (Turkish) conquerors centuries ago, by the way it was situated.

Sivershchyna [ˈsʲiːɥ ɪrʃtʃɪnɐ]
Region at the North, name of which derives from the Siveriany tribe, who populated the area at the Kyivan Rus times.

Podillia [pʊˈdʲiːlʲːɐ]
Region situated at the valley of the Pivdennyi Buh and the Dnister rivers, as if at the bottom ("podil" — bottom of something).

The Carpathians [kɑːrˈpeɪθjənz]
Commonly used name — The Carpathian Mountains.
Mountain region and the West of Ukraine. It covers Lemkivshchyna, Boikivshchyna and Hutsulshchyna, the regions of mountain ethnical groups of Ukrainians.

Bukovyna [bʊkʊˈɥɪnɐ]
Region at the West, the name of which derives from the Slavic word "buk" (Ukrainian: бук — beech) and means "beech forest" or "beech land".

Tavria [ˈtɑwrʲɒ]
Region at the South, washed by the Black sea, covers the Southern part of mainland Ukraine and the Crimean peninsula. The name of the region derives from the ancient tribe of Tavrs that lived here.

Prychornomoria [prɪˌtʃɔrnɒˈmɔːrʲɒ]
Commonly used name — The Black Sea Region.
Region is situated by (Ukrainian: при, "pry") the Black sea, at its Northern coast.

Naddniprianshchyna [nɒd̪ːnʲɪˈprʲanʲʃtʃɪnɒ]
Commonly used name — Dnieper Ukraine.
Central region, situated in the upper valley, as if over (Ukrainian: над, "nad") the Dnipro river.

Podniprovia and Zaporizhzhia [pʊd̪ːnʲɪˈprɔːwʲɒ] [zɒpʊˈrʲiʒʲːɒ]
Commonly used name — The Dnipro and Zaporizhzhia Steppes.
Steppe region, situated behind the rapids (Ukrainian: porohy) of the Dnipro river.

Volyn [wʊˈlɪnʲ]
Region at the North-West, the name of which derives from the name of the ancient Volyn city.

Slobozhanshchyna [slʊbɔˈʒɑːnʲʃtʃɪnɒ]
Commonly used name - Sloboda Ukraine.
Region named after the type of settlement "sloboda" — a big village or town — which were spread in the region many years ago.

Halychyna [ɦɑlɪtʃɪˈnɑː]
Commonly used name — Galicia.
Region at the West, the name of which derives from ancient Halych city, once the capital of the Kingdom of Galicia.

Volunteers, who took part in the project between June 2016 and July 2019:

Aleksandr Maiorov

Aleksandr Sirota

Aleksey Sobchuk

Alexander Legostaev

Alexandra Baklanova

Oleksii

Alexey Panchenko

Alina Kobernik

Alina Kondratenko

Alina Rudya

Alisa Smyrna

Alla Mandziuk

Alona Kabaliuk

Anastasia Koberska

Anastasiia
Matviets

Anastasiia Baklytska

Anastasiia Yakubyshyn

Anastasiya Blazhko

Andrew Sacheva

Andrii Bozhok

Andrii Illin

Andrii Kuzminskyi

Andrii Rohozin

Andrii Sydoruk

Andrii Zavertanyi

Andriy Bocharov

Ania Yabluchna

Anka Yemelyanova

Ann Ivanova

Anna Kubareva

Anna Chapala

Anna Dragula

Anna Holban

Anna Kondratyuk

Anna Lukasevych

Anna Maniati

Anna Vorobiova

Anna Yemelianova

Anton Protsiuk

Anton Shynkarenko

Anton Veklenko

Artem Halkin

Artem Rusko

Artem Zubkevych

Bogdan Logvynenko

Bogdan Suiunbaiev

Bogdana Korogod

Bohdan Lopatiy

Bohdanna Kapitsa

Bohdanna Korohod

Britta Ellwanger

Claire Little

Daniel Mecineanu

Daria Salo

Daria Temerbek

Daryna Ariamnova

Daryna Kyrychok

Dasha Pyrogova

Denys Antonchyk

Denys Bloshchynskyi

Diana Butsko

Diana Dalkevych

Diana Horban

Diana Staretska

Dmitriy Bartosh

Dmytro Bezverbnyi

Dmytro Chernenko

Dmytro Kosheliuk

Dmytro Koshevyi

Dmytro Okhrimenko

Dorina Gakman

Elina Foinska

Evgen Madenov

Francesco Pagano

Gayana Mkrtchyan

Halya Kohuch

Halyna Kurdiukova

Hanna Ostroverkha

Hanna Tymets

Hari Krisshnan

Helen Ivashenko

Iaroslava Kravchenko

Ihor Bukalo

Illia Suprun

Ilona Badenko

Ilona Mykolaishyn

Inna Parfeniuk

Inna Sakhno

Ira Stepanova

Ira Zhukevych

Iren Nosova

Iryna Burtyk

Iryna Hlushkevych

Iryna Oparina

Iryna Pelts

Iryna Shvets

Iryna Voloshyna

Iulia Fedorovych

Iuliia Rublevska

Ivan Shegda

Ivanna Zarytska

Jurii Stephanyak

Justyna Blaszczak

Kaitlin Vitt

Karina Piliugina

Karyna Mykytiuk

Kateryna Dashko

Kateryna Kapra

Kateryna Kulykova

Kateryna Lehka

Kateryna Senchenko

Kateryna Smuk

Katya Akvarelna

Katya Keretsman

Khrystyna Arkhytka

Khrystyna Bunii

Khrystyna Kulakovska

Khrystyna Oryshchak

Khrystyna Tynkalyuk

Kira Vereshchagina

Kostia Balytskyi

Ksenia Stetsenko

Kseniia Bundziak

Ksenya Riznyk

Lasha Avkopashvili

Lesia Diak

Lesya Homyak

Lesyk Yakymchuk

Liliya Yurkiv

Lina Golovnya

Lisa Litvinenko

Liuda Kravchenko

Liza Koshevaia

Lyuda Kucher

Maddalena Mongera	Natalia Petrynska	Olga Teslenko
Maks Kenig	Natalia Stec	Olga tsvetkova
Maksym Sytnikov	Natalia Vyshynska	Olha Dmytruk
Malanka Junko	Natalia Zinevych	Olha Glady
Maria Babchuk	Natálie Dubanevicová	Olha Honzajk
Maria Fomenko	Nataliia Bortnik	Olha Khanas
Maria Kolesnik	Nataliia Serediuk	Olha Kovalchuk
Maria Kovalchuk	Natalka Kursyk	Olha Reshetnyk
Maria Petrenko	Natasha Ponedilok	Olha Salimonovych
Maria Prokhorenko	Nazar Matvieichev	Olha Shcherbak
Maria Terebus	Nazar Omelyanovych	Olha Shevchenko
Mariana Kizlyk	Ndiya Rychok	Olha Stonozhenko
Marichka Kurylo-Aleksevych	Nick Zavilinskyi	Olha Stulii
Marichka Pohorilko	Nika Kreidenkova	Olia Chernyk
Marichka Ruban	Oksana Krasovska	Olia Diatel
Mariia Hlukh	Oksana Kuzema	Olia Zaverach
Mariia Shchur	Oleg Sologub	Ollie Shor
Mariia Zaichenko	Oleg Marchuk	Olya Tsuprykova
Marina Fudashkina	Oleg Pereverzev	Olya Zaverach
Mariya Maksimenkova	Oleksandr Bielov	Ondrej Cerný
Marta Burdiak	Oleksandr Horobets	Orest Rybii
Marta Hrechyn	Oleksandr Kabanov	Paul Danyliv
Marta Shrubkovska	Oleksandr Khomenko	Pavlik Mudryi
Maryan Manko	Oleksandr Popko	Pavlo Haidai
Maryna Odnorog	Oleksandr Portian	Pavlo Pakhomeko
Maryna Plutenko	Oleksandr Ratushnyak	Pavlo Pashko
Maryna Riabykina	Oleksandr Rybii	Pjotr Hiebert
Maryna Sarazhyn	Oleksandr Sloboda	Polina Zabizhko
Mateusz Baj	Oleksandr Tartachnyi	Polina Zymina
Max Zavalya	Oleksandr Yudin	Polya Bondaruk
Michael Chumak	Oleksandra Kosior	Pylyp Dotsenko
Mikhail Tsitou	Oleksandra Kyryanova	Roman Hladkyh
Misha Shelest	Oleksandra Vlasiuk	Roman Lypak
Mykhailo Slobodian	Oleksii Karpovych	Ruslan Veselui
Mykola Korol	Oleksii Yudin	Sashko Sivchenko
Mykola Nosok	Oleksiy Obolensky	Sergey Korovayny
Myroslava Oliinyk	Olena Vavshko	Sergii Guzenkov
Nadija Kuryliak	Olena Logvynenko	Sergii Rodionov
Nadiya Krutynska	Olena Yermolenko	Sergiy Kucherenko
Natalia Kucheriava	Olesia Yedynak-Khoma	Sergiy Polezhaka
Natalia Hryniuk	Olexandra Tesliuk	Serhii Horbatiuk
Natalia Kiryakova	Olga Gavrylyuk	Serhii Husakov
Natalia Lysak	Olga Kovalova	Serhii Nemyrovskyi
Natalia Panchenko	Olga Nova	Serhii Sverdielov

Sofia Anzheliuk

Sofia Bazko

Sofia Kalash

Sofia Serhiichuk

Solomìa Granger Chabursky

Solomia Husak

Solomia Vonsul

Stanislav Bielyi

Stanislav Blanco

Svitlana Borshch

Svitlana Urum

Tania Kostyuk

Tania Tarasova

Tanya Rodionova

Taras Kovalchuk

Tetiana Khuk

Tetiana Okopna

Tetiana Pasichnyk

Trayan Muse

Trayan Mustyatse

Tymur Pliushch

Vadim Syrovoj

Vadym Kruk

Valentyn Kuzan

Valentyn Pugachov

Valeriya Didenko

Varvara Verbytska

Vasyl Goshovsky

Vasyl Salyha

Vasylyna Haran

Vctoria Solodka

Victor Artemenko

Victoria Redia

Victoria Sorochuk

Vika Volyanska

Viktor Kozak

Viktoria Sypukhina

Viktoriia Savitska

Vira Brezhneva

Vitaliy Zhylak

Vlad Tsovma

Yana Bilynets

Yana Bogdanova

Yana Konyk

Yaroslav Azhnyuk

Yaroslav Karpenko

Yelizaveta Koshevaya

Yevgeniia Haydamaka

Yevgeniia Sapozhnykova

Yevhen Hlibovytsky

Ylyzaveta Chernova

Yu Kostenko

Yulia Kabanets

Yulia Plysiuk

Yulian Khorunzhyi

Yuliia Kostrovska

Yuliia Balka

Yuliia Derevianchuk

Yuliia Dyminska

Yuliia Kochetova-Nabozhniak

Yuliia Teleshova

Yuliia Turbovets

Yura Palyvoda

Yurii Pyrch

УДК 91(477) (036)
U31

Ukraïner
Ukrainian Insider

Автор ідеї **Богдан Логвиненко**
Упорядники **Оксана Кузема,
Наталія Понеділок, Софія Анжелюк**
Фото на обкладинці **Василь Салига**

Головний редактор **Мар'яна Савка**
Відповідальні редактори **Ольга Ренн,
Євгенія Сапожникова**
Перекладачі **Яна Білинець, Олена Вавшко,
Вікторія Сорочук, Еліна Фоїнська**
Літературні редактори **Анастасія Матвієць,
Ольга Ковальова, Брітта Еллвангер**
Пруфрідерка **Кейтлін Вітт, Галина Гринь**
Художній редактор **Назар Гайдучик**
Редактор фото **Олександр Хоменко**
Дизайн **Яся Богданова, Карина Микитюк**
Коректор **Марта Сахно**
Макетування **Тетяна Омельченко**
Шрифт **Кирило Ткачов**
Координатор **Людмила Кучер**

Original concept by **Bogdan Logvynenko**
Compilers **Oksana Kuzema, Natalia Ponedilok,
Sofia Anzheliuk**
Cover Photo **Vasyl Salyha**

Editor-in-Chief **Mariana Savka**
Senior Editors **Olga Renn,
Yevgeniia Sapozhnykova**
Translators **Yana Bilynets, Victoria Sorochuk,
Olena Vavshko, Elina Foinska**
Editors **Anastasiia Matviiets, Britta Ellwanger,
Olga Kovalova**
Proofreader **Kaitlin Vitt, Halyna Hryn**
Art editor **Nazar Haiduchyk**
Photo editor **Oleksandr Khomenko**
Designers **Yasia Bogdanova, Karyna Mykytiuk**
Layout engineer **Tanya Omelchenko**
Corrector **Marta Sakhno**
Font by **Kyrylo Tkachov**
Composition coordinator **Liudmyla Kucher**

Підписано до друку 02.09.2019.
Формат 70×90/16
Гарнітура: UA-brand. Друк офсетний.
Умовн. друк. арк. 28,37.
Наклад 3000 прим. Зам. № 185/08

Свідоцтво про внесення до
Державного реєстру видавців
ДК № 4708 від 09.04.2014 р.
Адреса для листування:
а/с 879, м. Львів, 79008

Львівський офіс:
вул. Старознесенська 24–26

Партнер видавництва

UNISOFT

Надруковано у ПП «Юнісофт»
61036, м.Харків, вул. Морозова, 13 б
www.unisoft.ua
Свідоцтво ДК №5747 від 06.11.2017 р.

Книжки «Видавництва Старого Лева»
Ви можете замовити на сайті www.starylev.com.ua
 0(800) 501 508   spilnota@starlev.com.ua

ISBN 978-617-679-731-9